Speed Reading 2022

The Best Guide to learning how to read a book of over 100 pages in 1 hour

Table of Contents

TABLE OF CONTENTS

INTRODUCTION

SECTION I – PRE-READING

    CHAPTER 1 – PURPOSE

    CHAPTER 2 – POWER OF PREVIEW

    CHAPTER 3 – CHANGE STYLES

SECTION II – SPEED READING TECHNIQUES

    CHAPTER 4 – SPACE READING

    CHAPTER 5 – CHUNKING

    CHAPTER 6 – SUBVOCALIZATION

SECTION III – ENHANCING THE TECHNIQUES

    CHAPTER 7 – FIXATION

    CHAPTER 8 – REGRESSION

    CHAPTER 9 – VISUAL RANGE

SECTION IV – IMPROVING COMPREHENSION

    CHAPTER 10 – READING FOR IDEAS OR MAIN POINTS

    CHAPTER 11 – TOPIC SENTENCES

    CHAPTER 12 – VOCABULARY

SECTION V – ADDITIONAL TIPS

    CHAPTER 13 – REMEMBERING WHAT YOU READ

CHAPTER 14 – VISUALIZE

CHAPTER 15 – EYE HEALTH

CONCLUSION

Introduction

The sheer volume of information the eyes take in at any moment is incomprehensible. Look around and take note of everything you see. If outside, notice the trees, cars, people, and everything in between. If sitting at a desk, take note of the pens, paper, notebook, and all the other material in front of you.

The mind processes these objects so fast you're not aware of the processing happen. You simply move your eyes in a direction, and they instantaneously detect and understand what is there.

When we read, however, things are not quite as smooth and fluid. It takes time and effort to process words, and the meaning conveyed by those words. For many, reading is a demanding activity that consumes a lot of mental energy. For some, it is so demanding, they avoid reading altogether.

So, the question is *why can't we process text the same way we process other objects in our environment*?

The truth is we can!

The human eye is an incredible organ. It is the second most complex organ in the body, containing 2 million components and 12 million photoreceptors. It functions faster and has a wider dynamic range than any camera. Brain scientists and information experts assert that up to 90 percent of the information we take in comes through the eyes.

The eyes do not operate alone but work in conjunction with the brain. In fact, the eyes are directly connected to the brain, which leads many to think they are an extension of the brain rather than distinct, separate organs. Scientists estimate that as much as 65 percent of the brain is used to process visual information.

If the eyes are the second most complex organ in the body, that makes the brain the *most* complex. In fact, many assert it is the most complex structure in the known universe - more complex than planets, stars, and even airplanes. The brain is behind our every thought, action, memory, feeling, and experience in the world.

So, humans are walking around with two of the world's most complex systems working together to provide the basic foundation of intelligence through observing, thinking, writing, and above all, reading. We have the natural ability to read and process information at a high level.

Unfortunately, most are simply not using this ability. That's because reading isn't something that originated in or exists in nature. Reading is something that humans created, and since it is manmade, it is not an instinctual skill that we are born to do. It is a skill that must be learned.

Most of us learn to read, but that doesn't mean we learn to read in the best way. Our educational systems and teachers, along with parents, do an admirable job of teaching us how to combine words to form sentences. However, they don't necessarily teach us the most effective way to use our impressive eyes and mind to do that. As a result, we are left feeling like we are not capable of reading better or faster.

This couldn't be further from the truth. The reality is, we *are* all capable of reading better and faster than we ever imagined. We simply need to learn the correct ways to use our infinitely powerful eyes and mind.

That is what this book aims to teach. With simple strategies that unleash the power of your mind and sight, the techniques in this book will fill in the gaps teachers failed to cover to accelerate reading in ways you can't imagine.

If you seek that level of improvement, continue reading.

The Process

Since the eyes and mind already have the ability to process information at a high level, this book doesn't require learning or doing anything new or difficult. All it requires is to make slight shifts in reading habits.

As a result, this book is not very lengthy or complicated. Each chapter is a few pages long and easy to read and digest. The chapters provide exactly what is needed to improve reading speed—and nothing more. The truth is, many of the important shifts in reading habits take only a few minutes to learn.

You can literally double or even triple current reading speed within minutes of reading some of the chapters and increase speed further after practicing the additional suggestions. With commitment, there is no doubt that you will develop the ability to read a 200+ page book in *one hour* !

Also, reading and comprehension go hand-in-hand, so in addition to improving reading speed, you will learn to improve comprehension. After all, the purpose of reading faster is to learn more information. What good is reading quickly if we can't make sense of and retain that information? Improving speed without improving comprehension is not speed reading. The goal is for you to read faster and with greater comprehension.

What's Inside

This book is divided into 5 sections. Each section has 3 chapters, and each chapter covers 1 aspect of the speed reading process.

Section I discusses what to do *before* beginning to read. Most people assume reading is only about picking up a book and reading words. That's an ineffective approach. There are important steps that precede the reading process, and the chapters in this section discuss these steps and explain why they are important.

Section II focuses on techniques that increase your ability to read more words in less time. That is, reading significantly more words in a significantly shorter amount of time. The techniques in this section are what people are searching when they seek to improve reading speed. It is the heart of the speed reading process and where those small shifts in habits that bring about the big results lie.

Section III expands on the techniques presented in Section II. It offers guidance on how to both enhance and refine the suggested techniques, all toward pushing reading speed even further. Committing to these chapters will push your ability to practically inhale information from written material.

Section IV is all about comprehension. Remember, reading without comprehension is not reading. This section presents strategies to better understand how authors organize written material and ways to use that knowledge to better understand their message. The material in this section also addresses creative ways to enhance vocabulary, a key element for both reading and comprehension.

Section V addresses topics that don't fit anywhere else. Although each chapter in this section stands on its own, each contains important lessons to enhance the reading experience, including improving memory, overcoming daydreaming, and maintaining eye health. This final section ties everything together.

This all may seem like a lot to take in, but trust me, it is not. Remember, each chapter is only a few pages, and majority of the advice is easy to read and understand. After understanding what to do, it is simply a matter of practice.

This brings up the next point:

Old Habits Die Hard

Although the lessons do not present significant learning challenges, where challenges may arise is in shifting reading habits. Habits are routines or behaviors that are repeated so often and for so long that they become automatic—and then permanent. Habits engage without conscious choice or decision, and often, they become the default action or response. Any behavior can become a habit, and that includes poor reading.

Habits can be difficult to break—extremely difficult. Even when a behavior isn't working and a better way exists, habits will keep you in them. Even if the alternative is the simplest technique, explained using the clearest instructions ever written, habits make it difficult to apply. Despite knowing what to do, and how to do it, old habits make it challenging to actually do it.

Such is the nature of habits. They are designed to keep you in a pattern, regardless of the benefit or pain they bring. Therefore, something as simple as shifting your eye gaze may at first feel like pulling teeth, creating intense amounts of resistance, discomfort, and even pain.

In order to effectively apply the instructions in this book, it is important to break free from old habits and adopt new ones. A great way to adopt new habits is with practice drills. Drills involve repeating a routine over and over, not in conjunction with any other activity, until the body develops a rhythm and *habit* for it.

Drills are key to successful skill development. High performers in many disciplines become high performers by regularly practicing their craft with drills. Practice drills are essential to learning, retaining, and most importantly, easing into doing something new.

For this reason, the chapters in this book end with practice drills that help you integrate and become accustomed to the instructions. I strongly recommend doing them before moving to the next chapter.

The mind and body learn and remember better from doing than from reading, hearing, or seeing. The sooner you start applying the techniques, the sooner you'll see improvements in reading. That means not only will these drills motivate you to begin using the techniques, but they will maximize learning.

Also, these drills build on one another. For example, the drill in one chapter instructs practicing one technique, while the drill in the next chapter instructs practicing another technique in combination with the first. In a subsequent chapter, you'll then practice the three together.

This cumulative approach trains you to use these techniques simultaneously. This way you can learn, understand, and physically integrate all the lessons by the time you finish the book. After finishing, you can jump to speed reading other material instead of starting at square one.

The drills presented in this book are simple and brief, each requiring 5 to 20 minutes to complete. Working through them will make a huge impact on your ability to learn and integrate the information. If you skip the drills, you will experience difficulty with the techniques and ultimately not form the necessary habits to use them.

People falsely assume they can take what they read and automatically apply it. That's wishful thinking. In order to apply the techniques, you need to apply the techniques, and these drills help you do that. With that said, don't skip any of the them. They are the most important part of this book.

Many of the drills involve practicing on various types of materials. So, before reading further, gather as many different types of written content as possible —everything from stories, novels, narratives, and articles to textbooks, manuals, newspapers, biographies, and trade journals to a variety of magazines, such as fashion, business, and special interest. Keep these materials at arm's length while reading this book, so when you arrive at a drill, you can start right away.

It might help to go to a library or book store, since all this material will be in close proximity. If that's not possible, work with what is available in the immediate environment.

With everything out of the way, let's begin developing the skill to read a 200+ page book in 1 hour.

Section I – Pre-Reading

Chapter 1 – Purpose

The two most important days in your life are the day you are born and the day you find out why—Mark Twain.

As noted in the introduction, reading isn't about jumping into a book the moment you pick it up. Important steps precede the reading process that aid in absorbing the text. The three chapters in this section discuss these steps, starting with *purpose* .

Have you ever noticed when you're in the market for a new car and have settled on a model to buy, you suddenly begin seeing that model everywhere? Or when setting a goal, opportunities related to that goal and ways to achieve it begin appearing all over?

This happens because the mind is a goal seeking, purpose driven machine. Setting a goal or purpose activates different neural networks and regions of the brain to work in unison. So, each region of the brain is not just doing its own thing. With purpose, the focus of the mind changes and its awareness opens, often without you realizing.

This is why new opportunities begin appearing. Of course, those same opportunities existed prior to setting the goal, but since they were of no interest at the time, the mind paid them no attention.

In addition to achieve goals, numerous well-documented studies show that purpose offers a host of physical, mental, and emotional benefits. Purpose in a person's life reduces the risk and the effects of many illnesses, including heart attack, stroke, Alzheimer's, depression, addiction, suicide, and anxiety.

Purpose improves mental function, increases concentration, and actually repairs the DNA. When people have purpose, they live longer, are happier, and have an easier time handling challenges, finding solutions, managing conflicts, using resources, and most importantly, living with a sense of belonging and well-being.

Purpose has power!

Purpose has power with reading as well. When a goal or purpose is applied to a reading assignment, the mind suddenly stops wandering, and instead, becomes focused on the material at hand. This makes you more attentive and less distracted, so you can get through a passage in less time and with less effort.

Since purpose has such power, the next time you sit down to read, set a goal or purpose. Determine beforehand what you want or hope to gain from the material.

Interestingly, we all have a purpose when reading. Anytime we pick up a book, magazine, or article, it's for a reason. The reason might be to ace an exam, write a paper, or to complete an assignment. Maybe it's to find an answer, learn a skill, or solve a problem. Some read to end boredom or to unwind and get lost in a fantasy. Whatever the purpose, there is a purpose—even if you don't consciously recognize that purpose.

Now, just because you know the purpose, that doesn't mean your mind will know as well. We often assume that we are one with our minds. We believe that when we know what we want, our minds automatically know as well. Sadly, that isn't true.

In any given moment, we have hundreds or even thousands of wants, drives, and desires percolating inside. Our minds are sifting through all of these wants to figure out which one to pursue in the moment. *Should I message a friend, respond to the boss, watch a show , eat lunch , clean up , ask out a classmate , listen to music , or play outside?*

Clarifying your purpose helps the mind tremendously. Instead of deciding which of the hundred urges to follow, it has a clear directive. It knows what to tune out and where to turn its attention. In other words, if you want your mind to know and pursue your goals and intentions, you must identify and clearly state them.

Anytime you pick up something to read, state the purpose or intention for reading it. The clearer the purpose, the easier it will be for the mind to interpret the information—and the faster you can sift through it.

Your purpose does not have to be long, drawn-out, or complicated. It can be as simple as *I'm reviewing yesterday's notes to find answers for tomorrow's assignment.* That's it.

The key is to determine why you are reading the text or what you want to know once finished. If reading for an assignment, you might ask why the instructor assigned the chapter or section. Two universal examples include: *What can I get out of this material* or *How will this reading help me* ?

Another option is to ask yourself specific questions that you'd like the material to answer. This option is easier with manuals and guide books, but can be applied to other materials as well.

The following are suggestions for different purposes you can set for a variety of materials:

• *I am reading this book to learn money-saving strategies to will help me grow my business.*

• *I am studying chapters 4, 5, and 6 of the history textbook to ace next week's mid-terms.*

• *My goal for reading this manual is to improve my computer programming skills for the new project at work.*

• *I am reading this novel to prepare for tomorrow's literature discussion.*

• *I am reviewing this book to learn all the facts I need to write an engaging research paper deserving of an A.*

• *The purpose of reading for the next few hours is to unwind, relax, and get lost in the author's tale.*

• I am researching the internet to find a better treatment option for my illness.

These examples illustrate how to define and state purpose. When you can't think of any on your own, feel free to borrow one from this list. Use it as is or modify it to fit the current situation or need.

Sometimes, it's annoying to step back and set a purpose, and have to do so every time you sit down to read. I'm sure you would rather just get started, because the sooner you start, the sooner you will finish.

Sure, setting purpose takes time but very little time. It shouldn't take longer than a few seconds to one minute to state a clear, meaningful objective. The short time that is spent will, in turn, help you get more from the reading, which will, ultimately, save considerably *more time* in the long run.

Practice Drill

For this drill, take out a blank sheet of paper.

1. Write down all the types of material you have read in the past. Note anything and everything, whether it was a sports magazine, internet article, Twitter post, history book, or science report. Don't limit the material to what was read in the *recent* past—go as far back as possible.

After writing down everything you can remember, next to each item, record your reason for reading that piece. Think about the reasons this chapter described earlier. Whatever they are, note them down.

2. Next, compile a list of all the reading you have planned in the next week, whether for school, work, or leisure. Next to these items, again cite the purpose.

3. Repeat step 2 for everything you expect to read in the next month. For students, this should be straightforward since most teachers and professors provide a course syllabus with the required reading outlined. For others, think about books you intend to buy, courses you plan to attend, topics you hope to

learn, skills you seek to develop, or job assignments you expect to receive.

Once again, think about the motivation for reading each of these items. What do you hope to get out of the material? Even if it is painstakingly obvious, write it down.

Make sure to be detailed and descriptive. Don't simply write, the purpose for reading the report is *to not get fired*. A better alternative might be: *to understand the client's logistic requirements to streamline their delivery* . Write in such a way that would allow someone who doesn't know you to clearly understand the motivation.

4. Repeat step 2 one more time for materials you are likely to come across in the next year.

Completing the 4 steps will provide you with a list of purposes for just about any material you encounter in the future. When reaching for something to read, you won't have to deal with the frustration of thinking about the objective. Instead, you can simply reference what arose in this drill, and either modify it or use it as is. This will not only save time, but also the headache that comes with trying to identify a clear purpose.

Purpose is valuable because it helps us determine what we want to get out of reading. Once we know, we can examine the reading to see if it will meet our goal. If it does not, a great deal of time is saved right away. So, what is a good way to examine a written piece to see if it meets a given purpose? We discuss this in the next chapter.

Chapter 2 – Power of Preview

Imagination is everything. It is the preview of life's coming attractions—
Albert Einstein

Several years ago, while traveling in Belize, I met a fellow traveler, a Canadian woman who had a particular habit. Whenever she arrived in a new city or town, the first thing she did was take a few hours to walk around and explore. She had to do that; otherwise, she would get anxious and restless.

We ended up traveling together, so whenever we arrived in a new town, we dropped our bags at the hotel and explored the town or neighborhood. It was an interesting experience. Taking on her practice made me feel as if I had done something worthwhile, because it gave me a useful preview of the town. I gained a better understanding of what to do, where to go, how to get there, and what the locals were like.

Since then, I've made her habit my own. The first thing I do in a new place is walk around and explore for a few hours. This really sets my expectations of what there is to do, and how much time I need or want to spend in that place.

This is how I want you to approach reading. I want you to preview material before reading it. That means scrolling through the text, scanning the table of contents, major headings, any words in bold or italics, visual aids, and any information that seems important.

Preview is one of the most important steps readers can take to improve reading speed and comprehension. That's because previewing gives the mind a framework of what will be discussed. This helps the mind understand the type of information that will be presented and how it will be organized.

It may not seem like a big deal to you, but to the mind, it's huge. It's like giving it the box cover of a jigsaw puzzle. Assembling a puzzle without the cover is time consuming and difficult. With the cover, you can see the big picture, so it's easier to figure out where the pieces go and how they fit.

The same principal applies to previewing what you read. It helps the mind see all the pieces and understand how they come together. As a result, you can quickly make sense of the material.

More importantly, previewing helps the mind make more accurate *predictions* about what is being read. Let's examine why this is important. Scientists constantly rave about how the human brain is so complex and powerful that we are *decades* away from building a computer that can do everything the brain can do. Even the introduction of this book touts the amazing power of the brain.

If the brain is so complex and powerful, why does it, and hence, why do we make mistakes? Humans are by no means perfect. Countless quotes speak of our erroneous nature, such as *To err is human* .

One reason is that the mind doesn't necessarily respond to what is happening in real time, but to what it thinks is *going* to happen. In other words, the mind is continually making predictions about the future.

Have you ever been in conversation and sensed what the other person was about to say before he or she said it? Have you watched a movie or read a story and somehow knew how it would end? Or perhaps you've had a feeling, hunch, or intuition about something that later came true?

These experiences occur because the mind is perpetually preparing for the unexpected—such as a predator jumping out at you. If you can react to a dangerous event before it happens, you are likely to survive it. At the same time, if you can anticipate an opportunity before the competition, you can take advantage of it. So, it is extremely useful to make snap judgments about the environment and to act on those judgments.

In order to do that, the mind makes predictions from a series of clues. It acts and reacts based on those predictions rather than on reality. In other words, we respond to people not based on what they are saying, but on what we assume they are going to say. We react to situations not based on the outcome, but rather on our fear and anticipation of the outcome. And we respond not based on the actual question someone asks, but on the question the mind *believes* is being asked. When our predictions are wrong, mistakes occur.

This happens in reading as well. When reading, the mind is constantly predicting what will come next. Whether or not we are aware of these predictions, they are there, occurring in the background. This means that we interpret what we read not always based on the actual text, but often on what our mind predicts the text is going to say—sometimes based on what the mind wants the text to say.

This is why proofreaders are taught to spell check by reading backward. When reading forward, the mind can guess, based on the context of the sentence or paragraph, the word that should come next. Therefore, we see words as they should be, not as they are. As a result, we increase the likelihood of overlooking spelling and grammatical errors.

The benefit of predicting what comes next is that you can read faster. There's no need to dissect every word, sentence, and paragraph with a fine-tooth comb to acquire meaning. Based on the author, topic, writing style, content, and other clues, your mental processes can simultaneously read and comprehend.

This is where preview is valuable. Preview helps the mind make accurate predictions. It allows the mind to see what the text is about, determine its length, and assess the writing style. And in the background, it can begin thinking about the material and the possible directions it can go.

While reading, the mind will reference what it learned from preview to confirm that its predictions reflect the actual content. This not only translates into faster reading, but better comprehension.

Skilled readers almost never read a text *cold* . Instead, they examine it first with preview. This allows them to begin with a great deal of information already processed. As a result, their mind is not guessing or worrying about what comes next. It can relax and concentrate on what is being read.

So, whether you're about to read an article, report, manual, novel, or chapter from a textbook, preview it before reading. You will experience a greater level of comprehension and may even increase speed.

Preview Guidelines

It is important to note that different materials require different approaches to preview. Books and manuals tend to be involved, so they demand extra time at this stage. Articles and reports, on the other hand, are usually shorter and more straightforward, so they do not require as much effort. In a previous book, I summarized preview guidelines that readers found useful, so I've included them here.

Articles and Reports

Read the first and last paragraphs, examine words in bold or italics, read any quoted texts, and glance at any illustrations.

Books and Manuals

Read the front and back covers. Review the table of contents to get a feel for organization, and notice if the book is divided into sections or parts. Read chapter headings to get a sense of the topics that will be covered.

Next, read samples of the text. If there is a preface, begin there. Read also the full introduction and conclusion. Finally, skim through the book and take note of items in bold, italics, quotes, and any diagrams or tables. While skimming, read the first and last paragraphs of each chapter.

Textbooks

The approach to previewing textbooks is similar to books and manuals, though in all likelihood, you'll be reading a textbook for a class. This means that the reading will be assigned one chapter at a time—or even one subheading at a time. So instead of previewing the entire textbook, focus only on the portion that is assigned.

Begin with the chapter objectives, then read the summaries at the start of each chapter. Most textbooks have review questions at the end of each chapter or section; read these and keep them in mind. As always, examine any and all items in bold, italics, quotes, as well as all illustrations and graphs.

Stories & Novels

Students always ask if it is necessary to preview stories or novels. The answer is, it depends. If reading a story or novel for pleasure, you may want to avoid any sort of preview; otherwise, you'll uncover too much of the plot, or worse, the ending. This takes away from the joy of reading such material.

On the other hand, if reading a story or novel as an assignment for class, especially if your knowledge and understanding will be tested, then it's beneficial to preview. In these instances, approach preview like any other material: read the front and back covers. Review the table of contents. Skim through the text. This type of material is unlikely to have items in bold or italics, or many illustrations or graphs, so instead, pay attention to the plot, setting, characters, and the roles they play.

These are some guidelines on how to approach preview with different types of material. In addition to these guidelines, it might help to identify sections or topics to which the author devotes the most amount of time and space as they are likely be valuable. The topics that use visual aids are also likely to be important. You might also analyze the *type* of writing—academic or general audience—and even the difficulty of the text. Allow the mind to absorb as much information about the material as possible.

To remember all this, think of T.H.I.E.V.E.S:

• **T** itle

• **H** eadings

• **I** ntroduction

• **E** very word in bold, underline, quote, and italics

- **V** isuals Aids

- **E** nd of Chapter Questions

- **S** ummary/Conclusion

Since preview is only a preparation step, do not spend too much time at this stage. The goal of preview is to sample the material, not get caught up in the details.

Therefore, spend no more than 45 seconds to 5 minutes. Typically, this means 45 seconds to 1 minute for shorter items like articles and reports, and 3 to 5 minutes for lengthier ones, such as books and manuals.

As with stating a purpose, you may feel that preview goes against the goal of speed reading. That is, the time spent on preview is time that could be used for reading, so valuable time is wasted previewing material you plan to read anyway. Therefore, you may skip preview, reasoning *This is a short article, in the time it takes to preview, I can be done with it* .

Whether you preview or not, the mind is going to make predictions. You can't stop this process. It is hardwired into the brain. By skipping preview, the mind is likely to make inaccurate predictions, making it difficult to understand the material.

Those who experience difficulty reading do so simply because the material is saying something different from what their mind is expecting it to say. The mind is expecting the subject to go in one direction; when in reality, it's going somewhere completely different. This disconnect causes a gap in understanding. The wider the gap between the prediction and actual content, the tougher it is to read and comprehend.

As defined in the intro, speed reading isn't about how fast one moves through text but how fast the facts and ideas can be comprehended. So yes, it is possible to speed through text without preview, but comprehension will suffer. The time saved comes at a cost, so it's just best to preview.

Another point to address is that at times, preview may not always help you gain a stronger grasp of the material. In some cases, preview may actually leave you confused. And that's to be expected.

Again, preview is not necessarily meant for you but rather for your mind. Any given material on any given topic can go in a million directions. An article about galaxies, for example, can discuss an assortment of facts since so much has been discovered about the topic. Preview helps the mind zero in on all the options. The mind may not guess exactly what's going to be discussed, but through preview, it can eliminate a million different possibilities. Eliminating possibilities is essential for accurate predictions.

Finally, preview can help determine if the text will meet the goal or purpose you established in Chapter 1. Based on the info you gather, you can determine if the material will contain the information or answers you seek. If so, you can proceed with confidence. If not, then you've saved a great deal of time.

If after preview, you are still unsure whether the material will meet the purpose, you might delve deeper into the preview process or begin reading with a little caution. If time is limited, skip the sections to which the least amount of space is devoted or where redundant information exists. Of course, also skip what you already know and read only the new information that you need.

Preview Drill

The introduction asked you to collect various types of reading materials, such as articles, novels, reports, and books. If you haven't already, please do so now as they will be required for this and subsequent drills.

Practice previewing each type of material you gathered. Don't read through any of them yet; just focus on the preview step. Pick an article. Then, read the title, author, first and last paragraphs, scan through the body for words in bold, italics, underline, and any illustrations, such as graphs, charts, and diagrams. Briefly consider what you might learn from the article and the overall message the author is trying to convey.

After previewing the article, pick something else, such as a book. Books are lengthier, so start with the summary and blurb on the back cover. From there, review the table of contents, paying careful attention to the chapter titles and subheadings. Next, read the first and last chapters, and finally, scan through the content for important information, or anything else that catches the eye.

Continue with the rest of the materials. Preview one. When you are done, preview the next. After completing the next, preview another after that. Habituate yourself to go straight to preview anytime you pick up something to read.

Anytime you have the urge to start without preview, practice resisting that urge. No matter how quickly the mind wants to get started, refrain yourself. If necessary, put the book down until the urge subsides. Condition your brain and habits to understand that it's not okay to proceed without preview. Let them know not to push you into reading without this important step.

Preview is important, but equally important is the manner in which you choose to read. All content is not created equal, and that's what we'll discuss next.

Chapter 3 – Change Styles

Some books are to be tasted, others to be swallowed, and some few to be chewed and digested –Francis Bacon

When it comes to reading, there is no one-size-fits-all approach. Not all material is meant to be read the same way. Not all material can be read the same way. Some are challenging, while others prove much easier to read.

In addition, your initial understanding of a subject plays a big role in how quickly it can be read. New or unfamiliar topics, no matter how well written, will require you to reduce reading speed to grasp it fully. If the topic is familiar, you likely won't even notice that what you're reading is difficult.

Therefore, adjust reading speed according to the importance, form, genre, and difficulty of the material. In other words, don't read textbooks in the same way as email. And don't read email in the same way as a training manual. Each type of material presents its own challenges. Be aware of the challenges and adjust your speed accordingly.

You are probably thinking, *Well, this is obvious* .

Indeed, it is very obvious!

As obvious as it is, readers still read all material, across all types and genres, as if they were all the same.

The primary reason readers do this is habit. They become habituated to reading a certain way, especially if they consume the same type of content, such as novels or textbooks. Once people fall into a pattern, they apply that pattern to everything.

The action is not conscious—it just happens. As soon as we pick up a book, habit takes over, and we're in the habituated pattern. If our pattern of reading isn't the best fit for the book at hand, we have a hard time taking in or making sense of it. This causes us to assume that we are not cut out for the subject, topic, or information.

It's not that you are not cut out, it's just that you need to adjust the reading process. That means changing the speed at which you read, as well as the level of energy and attention you put forth while reading.

Don't assume that all works must be read in the same way or at the same speed. Also, don't feel bad that certain topics or subjects require you to slow down. It's in no way a reflection of your intelligence. It is okay to vary reading approach based on the material.

Guidelines

The following are guidelines on how you might approach different types of reading.

Technical

Let's start with technical manuals, which often present detailed instructions and procedures that must be carefully followed. This makes each line of text extremely important. Overlooking even one or two sentences can result in errors that lead to grave consequences. Therefore, curb any temptation to haphazardly coast over such works. Instead, carefully *chew* and *digest* each and every line.

The same applies to legal documents, annual reports, write-ups, and policies. These types of documents are better read in their entirety and given full attention and focus. Similarly, it's sensible to slow down if you have to teach the material to someone else. Even a love letter or poem might be worth slowing down for, so you can enjoy the prose in the way the writer intended.

Familiar

When reading material related to an academic major or profession, there's less need to be as careful. Nonetheless, remain careful enough to fully understand and retain the material. This can involve taking notes and stopping regularly to test your knowledge of the subject. The same applies if the text is complicated, filled with big words and fancy grammar, or if you are new to the subject.

On the other hand, if you are well versed in a topic, are already familiar with the writer's other work, or are accustomed to the genre, you can increase pace. Some people are used to reading textbooks; whether computer science or political science, they have no problem learning from such material. For others, textbooks are stale and boring, so they have to really change their pace and rhythm to stay engaged.

Pleasure

With material read for pleasure, you can be relaxed. There is no need to rush, but at the same time, no need to go slow. Read at a pace that feels comfortable and enjoyable in the moment.

This will vary depending on your mood. Some days, you'll feel like reading without worrying about what you learn, how much you take in, or how useful it will prove. Other days, you may find that absorbing every sensory detail or dissecting the meaning behind every word is more enjoyable.

At the same time, no need to force yourself to read each and every sentence; take in what you can and skip areas that offer little or no interest. Some delight in a leisurely perusal of the morning paper by selecting areas of interest while ignoring content that lacks appeal. If it's for pleasure, do what is pleasing.

Relevance

Something else worth considering is how long the information will remain relevant. If reading to find a solution to a problem, but once solved, you have no further use for the information, then there is no need to be so meticulous. On the other hand, if the information is essential to your major or occupation, or if it's indispensable in another area of life, such as health or finances, be thorough.

Also consider the level of knowledge you seek. Do you seek quick explanation, broad ideas, complete comprehension, or detailed analysis? It goes without saying that the more detailed and complete awareness you seek, the slower and more attentively you should read.

Foundational

Finally, always spend extra time on information that sets the foundation for complex or elaborate ideas. The natural inclination is to skim over such foundational content, because it tends to feel familiar or easy to grasp. However, if you skim over the basics, you will have difficulty reading and learning what comes later. Certain subjects are, indeed, cumulative!

This means pay extra attention to earlier parts of books, stories, and novels, as that's where the foundational elements are developed. Once you have a solid base, you can change pace as desired, which leads to the next point.

Pace

Some content requires switching pace frequently. Certain chapters or sections you'll read quickly. Other chapters, you'll hit a patch that is difficult or that you sense is important, so you slow down and read carefully. Then, you speed up again.

This is particularly true for research. Research requires reading a wide range of related materials to support or reject a claim, or to find a solution. When conducting research, many ideas will be familiar. In fact, ideas that appear in one source may also appear in several other sources. In these cases, race over the ideas that repeat and slow down for topics that are new or foreign.

With that said, speed reading isn't always about hitting cruise control or flooring the gas to reach maximum velocity. Sometimes, the road will backup, you'll hit a series of lights, or find yourself stuck in heavy traffic. Other times, you'll be in such a flow, it'll feel like you're on the open highway.

In summary, anytime you pick up a book or other reading material, don't just start reading it using your standard pattern. Take a moment to gauge the content and your purpose. Ask yourself the following questions:

- What am I trying to gain from the material—background information on a topic I know little about or specific details and facts to support an argument?

- How long will the information be relevant—for the moment, to clear a temporary hurdle, or for the foreseeable future of my profession?

- How difficult is the material to read and comprehend?

Based on your answers, adjust reading accordingly.

This is the reason the first two chapters on preview and purpose are so important, because they provide these insights. Carefully taking the prescribed steps outlined in Chapters 1 and 2 will immediately reveal the adjustments that need to be made to your reading.

Practice Drill

Take the materials you were asked to gather—the different reports, articles, and books—and read a few pages of each. Based on what you gathered from the preview step about the style, form, genre, and relevance, adjust your reading pace and rhythm.

If the text is challenging, read slowly. The same applies if the topic is new, unfamiliar, or if it is something you really want or need to remember. On the other hand, if the content proves boring, familiar, or easy to process, and digest, feel free to increase speed.

When doing this drill, alternate between excerpts that are easy and ones that are difficult. After sampling an easy one, read a difficult one. Then, return to an easy one. Alternating the difficulty like this gives you practice adjusting speed and rhythm.

Like most people, you will find it difficult to switch pace. Your habit wants to read all material at the one speed to which it has become accustomed, and going against the habit will create resistance.

And, if you are the type of person who is always on the go, you want to get through the material as quickly as possible, regardless of purpose or difficulty. You have no desire to slow down or adjust pace. Your only desire is to keep going and going. In fact, it may almost be impossible for you to slow down. Even knowing concepts are being missed, the old habits keep pushing you forward.

Resist this tendency. Work to shift pace to suit the style and difficulty of the material. Slow down if necessary, even if the resistance is great. If your natural inclination is to read slow, speed up to a pace that's slightly uncomfortable. Practice getting accustomed to reading at different speeds.

This concludes Section I on prereading—important steps that precede the reading process. In this section, you learned three activities one should do before beginning any reading task: define purpose, preview, and change reading style.

Section II – Speed Reading Techniques

Chapter 4 – Space Reading ®

Beyond the edge of the world there's a space where emptiness and substance neatly overlap –Haruki Murakami

Section I discussed the formalities of speed reading—foundational steps that precede reading. Although these steps don't *directly* raise speed, they are important to the process.

This section presents techniques that directly impact reading speed and ability. As noted in the introduction, it focuses on increasing one's ability to read more words in a shorter time. This section will be the *meat* of the book, where you will learn to glide through text quicker and easier.

In order for these techniques to make sense, it helps to understand an important feature of the eye. The eye has the ability to process an image or object both as a whole and as a collection of individual parts. When looking at a friend's face, for example, the eyes and mind process the face as a whole rather than looking at individual parts, such as eyes, mouth, nose, and all the other minute features. This allows you to recognize the friend immediately. At the same time, if you wanted to focus on the individual features, you could do that as well.

Though, what would happen if you did focus on a single feature of your friend, such as an eyelash, nostril, or dimple? Narrowing vision to such a minute detail would hinder the ability to recognize the person. Such a restricted focus would require scanning other parts of the face and then putting all those parts together to recognize that individual.

This is how most of us read; we narrow our focus to each word or letter. Much like understanding a face, this process forces us to read bit by bit—letter by letter or word by word—to absorb any significant meaning. If we are distracted or our mind wanders, we miss the meaning of the entire sentence or paragraph and must start over.

This is not an effective way to read since, as you now know, the eyes and mind have the ability to see and process much more in a single glance. The solution, therefore, is to not focus on single words but rather to expand visual awareness and see groups of words at one time. This is the natural way the mind absorbs information from sight.

There are two ways to look at groups of words. The first method, which I call Space Reading ® , will be covered in this chapter. Space Reading directs you to avoid looking at the words you are reading, but rather at the spaces in between the words. That's right—at the spaces between words!

You're probably wondering, ***how the heck will looking at the spaces between words improve reading speed and comprehension*** ? To understand the answer, it helps to understand how I discovered the technique.

Since the mind and eyes have the ability to process information from sight extremely fast, I thought, *why should reading be any different* ? I began thinking, there's got to be a way to process written information like how we process everything else from sight.

That led me on a quest. I scoured the internet for reading systems, researched everything about how the eyes work, and even experimented with different ways of reading – looking at the top half of words, the bottom half, skipping words, looking at only the sides, and on and on.

One day, I began looking at the spaces between every 3-4 words, and voila, the technique was born! That is, paying attention to the white space prevents the eyes from narrowing their focus, and thus, fixating on individual words. As a result, the eyes can pick up more information, just as when they look at a someone's face.

It's easy to spend hours explaining the whys and hows of this phenomenon with studies to back up the claim; however, it will be much easier to show you firsthand. Below is a two-sentence paragraph with a small dot in between each word. Scroll through the paragraph by glancing at each of the dots. Start with the first dot, then move to the second, third, and so on. Don't look at the words to the right or left of the dot—simply move your eyes from one dot to the next, and do so in quick succession.

Even · though · you · are · not · looking · at · any · of · the · words · in · this · par eyes · and · mind · are · still · able · to · pick · up · the · text. · This · happens · b attention · to · the · spaces · prevents · your · eyes · from · narrowing · their · foc individual · words.

Amazing, right?

By focusing only on the dots—the spaces between the words—the mind was able to rapidly capture the text. As a result, you were able to read more, at a faster speed, and with greater comprehension. If you were unable to pick up the text, try this exercise again. Remember, simply look at the dots in between the words, and move swiftly from one dot to the next.

That's all!

Just as when you look at a tree, a car, or anything else in the environment, the mind picks up the information without you having to think about or work at it. That's what your marvelous eyes and brain are designed to do!

Then, to read faster, transition from looking at the spaces between every two words to looking at the spaces between every three words. Then every four words. With enough practice, you can advance to looking at only a few spaces per row of text to quickly grasp the information in that row.

Let's try the exercise again with the dots spaced between every three words. Below is the same paragraph as above, but with dots between every three words. As before, bounce your eyes from one dot to the next in quick succession.

Even though you · are not looking · at individual words · in this paragraph · yo eyes and mind · are still able to · pick up the text · This happens because · payi attention to · spaces between words · prevents your eyes · from narrowing thei focus · on individual words.

This is the essence of speed reading, you grab text as a whole instead of in individual parts. When using this technique, don't analyze, evaluate, or verbalize the text either aloud or in your head. Simply maintain a steady rhythm and skim left to right across each sentence, from one blank space to the next, without stopping or trying to make sure you understand what is being said.

With enough practice, you can raise your speed so you only need to look at a few spaces per line of text to grasp the information in that line, and do so with higher attention and comprehension

However, don't immediately jump to this level. Practice first with a space between every two words. Once comfortable there, move up to glancing at spaces between every three words. Move up to one space every four words only when you are proficient with three. You will eventually reach a level where you can absorb an entire sentence by merely glancing at two spaces, one in the middle-left and then the middle-right.

As you progress, make sure to work on expanding peripheral vision. That is, expand the ability to capture more words to the left and right of the space. The goal is to notice more and more words on each side. This will be discussed further in chapter 9.

Some people advance to such a level that they need glance only at one space —the one in the middle—to capture the entire line of text. They read by moving down one row to the next, gazing only at the space in the middle of each line.

If you didn't see the magic in this or were unable to pick up the text the first time, try the exercise again. Remember, look only at the dots in between the words in the above paragraph, and move swiftly from one dot to the next. This time, try softening your gaze a bit.

In the beginning, avoid the need to comprehend what you are reading. Simply focus on developing the habit of looking at the spaces and moving from one space to the next. Understanding and comprehension will come naturally since the mind evolved to derive meaning from information the eyes take in. Trust the mind to construct meaning without conscious effort on your part.

The great thing about this technique is that it is not a skill that needs to be learned or developed; it is an innate ability that you already possess. It's the natural way the eyes and mind work to process information. Therefore, you need only change the habit from looking at words to looking at the spaces *between* those words.

Which brings us to the . . .

Practice Drill

This drill will train the eyes to shift focus from looking at words to looking at spaces between words. To start, scroll back to the beginning of this chapter and reread it using the technique of Space Reading, which means moving the eyes from one blank space to the next without stopping. Remember not to analyze, evaluate, or try to make meaning. Your only goal right now is to bounce from one space to the next in quick succession.

After going through the chapter once, repeat the drill, but this time, move the eyes between spaces every two words. Make sure to do this through the entire chapter. It will go faster this time because you are stopping on fewer spaces. When you finish, begin again with every three words. Finally, reread the chapter while looking at spaces between every three words.

As you become comfortable, reread this chapter one more time, looking at spaces every four words while also trying to make sense of the words and their meaning. You might need to go slower, because now, you are actively involved in making sense of the content.

After completing this step, practice reading while looking at spaces every four words on the materials gathered for the previous drill—articles, reports, and even email and social media posts. Get the eyes accustomed to doing this with big text, small text, text with wide columns, and short columns.

Looking at spaces between words is one technique that directly impacts reading speed and ability. The next chapter will cover the second technique, called chunking. Both methods keep the eyes from fixating on individual words, so that you can naturally soak in more information (Please note: Space Reading® is trademarked and cannot be reproduced without prior express written permission).

Chapter 5 – Chunking

Looking at chunks is far better than looking at hunks –Kam Knight

In this chapter, you will learn another deceptively simple trick to boost reading called *chunking* . Unlike the previous technique of Space Reading, which focused on looking at the spaces in between words, chunking involves looking at the words themselves. However, instead of looking at words one at a time, you glance at groups, or *chunks,* of words.

Chunking works on the same principal as Space Reading. As you learned, the eyes have the ability to process an image or object either in its entirety or in distinct parts. When looking at a distinct part, the eyes instinctively focus in on that part to the exclusion of all others. This causes us to miss everything around it.

Consider what happens when a camera takes a picture of a close object. The background becomes blurred. Conversely, when there is no object in close view, the background is clear.

The same principle applies with our eyes. When we look at a word, the eyes' natural tendency is to narrow their field of vision to that one specific word, while disregarding the words around it. That leaves us no choice but to read text one word at a time.

Chunking opens our line of sight to capture more words in a single glance. The eyes are not set on a single word of a sentence, but instead, on a block, or chunk, of words in that sentence. You look at a chunk, move to another chunk, then another, and so on.

Let's look at an example. Below is a paragraph very much like the sample paragraph in the previous chapter. This time, the paragraph is separated into chunks with the "/" character. Position your eyes on the first chunk, and look at all the words together as a whole. Then, move the eyes to the next chunk and then the next in rapid sequence.

Even though you / are not looking / at individual words / in this paragraph / your eyes and mind / are still able / to pick up the text. / This happens because / paying attention to / chunks of words / prevents your eyes / from narrowing their focus / on individual words.

As with Space Reading, you were able to capture the text without focusing on individual words. And just as with Space Reading, you increased reading speed simply by changing the way you look at words. You may have thought that you wouldn't be able to read text more than one word at a time, but as you just experienced firsthand, the eyes and mind do, indeed, have the ability to grab a group of words in a single glance.

The key to this technique is not to grab words at random but to grab combinations that form a **phrase** . A phrase is two or more words that form a meaningful unit in a sentence. If you notice, the previous paragraph is broken into meaningful units: *In this paragraph* , *at individual words* , and *your eyes and mind* . These combinations have meaning, and such combinations help the mind pick up chunks as one large, meaning-rich word.

If possible, avoid combinations like:

/ this paragraph your eyes /

/ and mind are still /

/ the text. This happens. /

Such combinations are difficult to understand, and therefore, difficult to process. Consequently, they keep you from reaching your maximum potential. At the same time, there isn't only one correct phrase combination either: different people can select different chunks in any given sentence, which can still be classified as a phrase.

You've now learned two direct techniques to increase reading speed—Space Reading and chunking. Both techniques work on the same principal of softening the eye's gaze and moving over multiple words in a single glance.

Although both work on the same principal, they function independently of one another. That is, they can't necessarily be used together because it is difficult to effectively look at a space and chuck at the same time. When reading, you will either look at spaces or at chunks of words, **but not both** .

Since the two techniques operate independently, it is best to choose one to develop. Neither is right or wrong, neither is better or worse. Both techniques integrate well with the suggestions in later chapters.

It's really a matter of preference. Personally, I prefer Space Reading because it is easy and natural for me. All I have to do is think about spaces—and that's all. There is no strain or struggle. Though, you may feel that way about chunking.

The best way to determine which technique you prefer is to practice the drills in the two chapter. You might like both, finding that Space Reading works better with some types of material, while chunking works better with others, which is perfectly acceptable. Whichever you prefer, refrain from using both at the same time.

Practice Drill

This drill requires—you guessed it—rereading this chapter using chunking. First, reread the chapter chunking two words at a time. Then read it chunking three words at a time. Finally, four words at a time. With each pass, focus only on grabbing words in chunks and not on making sense of the words in the chunks.

Once you are comfortable grabbing chunks of four words, the next step is to pick out chunks that form phrases. This step may be challenging, so you may need to slow down considerably, even stopping to analyze whether a particular chunk makes up a phrase, or perhaps, a better combination exists.

Allow yourself to go as slowly as needed. It's what you and your mind need to get a feel for what makes good phrases. This is why these practice drills are important—they provide the breathing room to do that.

With consistent practice, you will find that picking out phrases becomes second nature. You will be able to do it with little effort; it will just happen. Still, you have to start somewhere, and there is no better place than with this drill.

Once you get the hang of picking out phrases, the final part of the drill is to read the chapter while making sense of how the phrases come together to form sentences and paragraphs. As before, take the exercise beyond this chapter and onto the other materials you pulled gathered.

As with anything in life, speed reading is about increasing habits that speed you up while decreasing habits that slow you down. So far, this section outlined two habits that speed up reading. Now, let's turn attention to a not-so-effective habit that slows it down.

Chapter 6 – Subvocalization

Think before you speak. Read before you think –Fran Lebowitz

This chapter trains you to break a habit called subvocalization, which alone can double or even triple reading speed. Subvocalization is the act of pronouncing every word that is read. When subvocalizing, you either *say* words out loud, *hear* them spoken in your mind, or *move* your lips to their pronunciation. Any one of these acts is subvocalizing.

Subvocalization greatly reduces the speed at which you read by adding an unnecessary step, or steps, to your reading. In addition to seeing the word, you are also hearing and/or speaking it.

The problem is that speech is a relatively slow activity. Our mind can't *say* words as fast as it can *see* them. This makes it impossible to read faster than we talk. By vocalizing words, out loud or in our head, we force the mind to read slower than its potential. Essentially, the mind is forced to perform two tasks at once.

Remember the exercise from the introduction, when asked to notice everything in the immediate environment, did you verbalize what you saw? Probably not. Or, do you verbalize everything you encounter while walking down the street? *That's a building , that's a side walk , and there's a street sign I see another building and now another street sign .*

Of course not.

Instead, we take in what the eyes capture without adding the additional step of vocalizing.

If you did stop to vocalize it all, imagine how long that would take. You would have to walk significantly slower to ensure you caught everything. It's the same when we vocalize while reading. Our pace is significantly reduced.

And slower reading isn't the only side-effect of subvocalization. When subvocalizing, we increase the chances of getting bored. Most of our inner thoughts are spoken in a monotone, expressionless manner, and subvocalizing is often done in the same manner. In other words, we tend to read in the same unexciting tone that we use when talking to ourselves.

As a result, the text just drones on and on inside our head, and before we know it, we're tired, uninterested, and perhaps, even starting to daydream. We might assume the material we were reading was causing that boredom, but in reality, the cause was simply the sound of our inner voice!

What's more, pronouncing every syllable of every word slows reading even further. Believe it or not, many readers actually take the time to carefully pronounce every word.

If unsure about whether you subvocalize, try this: while reading the next few paragraphs or pages in this book, notice whether or not your lips move, even slightly, or if you hear yourself say the words out loud. If you do either, you subvocalize. Though, don't be too hard on yourself, most people are guilty of this habit.

Subvocalization is a behavior that starts when we first learn to read, because we are taught to read phonetically. We read out loud to connect the right sound to the right word. This is necessary for the brain to learn the words and develop associations with those words.

Once we become fluent, we stop reading out loud but continue the phonetic process. We either start whispering these sounds in our mind or begin moving our lips so others can't hear us. Most people continue reading this way for the rest of their lives, hearing the little *voice* in the back of their mind and moving their lips to that voice.

Clearly at one point, vocalization was a necessary evil. However, once we've learned to read, subvocalization is no longer needed. Since the eyes and brain are capable of reading and comprehending all on their own, subvocalizing simply gets in the way of your true potential.

Also, as mentioned, information is received faster from sight than is received from hearing or speaking. Relying on sight alone immediately increases reading speed, because you go from glancing at words to directly understanding their meaning without any steps in between. As stated, simply by eliminating subvocalization, you can double or triple reading speed right here and right now.

Removing Subvocalization

As beneficial as it is to silence the *inner narrator* though, it's not easy. As you learned, it takes time and effort to break long-lasting habits. Nonetheless, the following suggestions reduce the difficulty.

Close Your Mouth

First and foremost, close your mouth when reading. Talking activates many parts of the body, such as the lips, mouth, tongue, jaw, and throat. Subvocalization does as well but to a lesser degree. Despite being less, it still affects speed.

Keeping the mouth closed disengages these processes, thus preventing you from saying the words out loud or moving your lips to their pronunciation. You'll be surprised how much this single, deliberate action can curb the urge to verbalize.

Read Faster than Speech

Read at a fast-enough pace where you simply cannot pronounce words or think about their sounds. Humans speak one word at a time and not three or four. Apply the suggestions in the last two chapters to grab multiple words between each space or chunk.

The more words you grab simultaneously, the more you disrupt the habit of sounding them out. Do this quickly. Move between spaces or chunks so fast that the part of you that needs to sound out or hear the words can't keep up.

Hum

Another option involves humming. Hum a tune, song, or a basic melody. Humming works because it preoccupies the vocal cords, so that you can't speak or whisper any words.

Humming also drowns out the voice in your head, along with any distracting noise in the immediate environment. If, for example, you are reading around noisy neighbors or loud machinery, humming can replace those annoying sounds with something more soothing.

As an added benefit, humming can set a rhythm and pace to your reading. To speed up reading, hum faster. If you are reading uncontrollably fast and need a way to slow down, hum slower. Humming is an effective way to control reading speed and pace.

The only drawback to humming is that in a public setting, it might distract or annoy others. In these situations, hum in your head; that is, imagine the sound of the humming. Or hum with your breath, breathing to the sound of the tune or song.

This is a slightly more difficult suggestion to master because it involves engaging in two unrelated activities: reading and humming. They are two activities you've likely never done together, so it may be challenging at first. But if you find humming effective, it's a skill worth developing. And as with any skill, consistent practice makes it second nature.

Music

The last and most popular option to break the subvocalization habit is to listen to music. Play it loud enough so that you can't hear yourself think, because if you can't hear yourself think, you won't be able to hear yourself read.

Research shows that music without words or lyrics, such as classical, instrumental, or electronic music, are the best options for reading. Lyrics in a song compete with words in a text for the mind's attention. Without lyrics, extraneous words aren't getting in the way.

These are some ways to eliminate subvocalization. They are not difficult to implement but do require shifting habits, which isn't always easy. By sticking to them, you will start reading faster almost immediately.

Practice Drill

Choose one of the speed reading techniques you learned in the last two chapters. Then, go to the beginning of this chapter, and as you space read or chunk through the material, tame the desire to subvocalize.

Begin by closing your mouth to adjust to reading without moving your lips. This will come naturally to those who already read this way, but for others, it will be a bigger struggle than it initially seems. After every few sentences, you may catch yourself unknowingly opening or moving your lips.

Each time you catch yourself subvocalizing, stop and close your mouth before moving forward. To really ingrain this habit, *any* time the lips part, return to the beginning and start the exercise again.

Once you are accustomed to reading with mouth closed, advance to reading without hearing or sounding out any words. Use the Space Reading or chunking techniques to move through the words quicker than you can speak them. To create an even larger *buffer*, try humming.

Don't worry just yet about comprehension but only about moving through the text without engaging the verbal or auditory senses. When you can comfortably space read or chunk without any form of vocalization, read the passages once again, this time for comprehension. Remember to carry the practice to the other materials.

This wraps up Section II on the specific speed reading techniques. Now that you know the techniques, let's discuss ways to enhance them, which we cover in the next section.

Section III – Enhancing the Techniques

Chapter 7 – Fixation

Perhaps all anxiety might derive from a fixation on moments –Sarah Manguso

Hopefully, you're realizing by now that speed reading isn't a demanding activity that requires enormous time, energy, and effort. The eyes and mind already possess the ability to read fast; all you need to do is break a few habits and make slight shifts in the way you look at words. Shifts such as looking at spaces, chunking, and reducing, or even eliminating the habit of subvocalization.

This section offers strategies to enhance and refine these techniques, which will, in turn, enhance and refine your reading speed and comprehension. As effective as the techniques in the previous chapters are, there are things you can do to make them even more effective.

The first involves reducing fixation. Though fixation sounds like a complex psychological disorder, it is simply the length of time the eyes stop and rest on a subject. Anytime we look at something, our eyes still themselves. This pause, called fixation, is the eyes' ability to stop moving so they can focus. If they didn't do this, everything in life would be a blur.

Fixation occurs during reading as well. When we read, our eyes stop and fix on words to see them clearly. They don't stop for long, but they do, indeed, stop with each and every word. This quick pause gives the eyes an opportunity to pick up the text.

In addition to fixating, the eyes also jump. As it relates to reading, the eyes jump from one word to the next. These jumps take place in between each fixation. As the eyes look at a word, they *fixate* . To look at the next word, they *jump* .

Our eyes are continually fixating and jumping, though it happens so fast that we don't realize it. When reading a 10-word sentence, your eyes will probably fixate and jump about 9 times.

To witness this process in action, close one of your eyes and place the tip of your index finger on the closed eye. With the open eye, slowly look left and right. You will actually feel distinct stop and go movements on the finger of the closed eye.

You can also observe fixation and jumping by watching others read. The next time you see someone immersed in a book, watch as their eyes move across the text. Notice that their eyes don't move smoothly; instead, their eyes make small, quick *pauses* and then *jumps* as they follow the line of print.

Since our eyes naturally stop to fixate on words, they present a mechanical barrier to speed reading. The fact that the eyes stop means, in that moment, they are unable to see the next word. Even though the pauses are for a split second, given the numbers of words in a document, they add up. The point is the more words we fixate on, and the longer we hold each fixation, the slower we read.

Fixation also reduces reading comprehension. Meaning is easier to pull from groups of words than from individual words or even single letters. Remember the face example from Chapter 4? It's difficult to make out a person's face by focusing on his or her individual features. The same is true with fixation during reading. The more you fixate on individual words, the more difficult it is to grab meaning from a sentence.

We falsely assume that slower reading means better comprehension. This may be true in some cases, but in most cases, the factors causing slower reading also cause lower comprehension. If you read slowly and still struggle with comprehension, you likely fixate too much.

Not to mention, fixation takes the fun out of reading. By fixating on every word in a sentence, it takes longer to get to the point the writer is trying to communicate. This creates impatience, lack of interest, and loss of focus. Losing focus causes comprehension to suffer further, and eventually, the desire to read altogether.

To increase reading speed and comprehension, it makes sense then to manage eye fixation. Although essential to reading—and to seeing in general—it can be reduced significantly.

There are two ways to do this. First, by reducing the number of words you fixate on. Second, by decreasing the length of time you hold each fixation. Let's explore both further.

Reduce Number of Fixations

The obvious way to reduce fixation is to pick up more words each time the eye stops. You learned to do this in the last section through Space Reading, chunking, and limiting subvocalization. These techniques were designed for this exact purpose.

To quickly review, with Space Reading, remember to skip as many words as possible between spaces. When chunking, fit as many words into each group or chunk. And because subvocalization means sounding out, hearing, or moving lips to each word, those who read this way have no choice but to fixate frequently, since the eyes must stop to verbalize each word before proceeding. Removing subvocalization means you are not forced to make so many stops.

Employing Space Reading or chunking and limiting subvocalization will significantly reduce the number of words on which you fixate. Rather than stopping on each and every word, you can expand the capacity to capture three to seven words, or more, in a single glance.

Reduce Length of Fixation

Another tactic to reduce the effects of fixation is to shorten the time the eyes spend on each pause or fixation. Instead of staying on a fixation for an extended period, continue moving the eyes forward when reading. Don't slow down to contemplate the text—just keep moving to the next space or chunk of words.

Whether on one word or groups of words, the average reader fixates 4 times each second. That means each fixation is a quarter of a second. If that can be reduced even by half, it in effect doubles speed.

Practice Drill

The previous drill had you practice Space Reading or chunking while limiting subvocalization. In this drill, you will do that again but with shorter fixations.

Return to the beginning of this chapter, and while using the technique of Space Reading or chunking, reread the chapter slightly quicker than you just did or perhaps faster than you are comfortable doing. Remember to keep lips sealed and refrain from any form of subvocalization.

Then read the chapter again at a little faster pace. Look at the same number of words, but move faster than before. Reread a third time at a slightly faster pace. As before, don't worry about making sense of the material; simply foster the habit of reducing the amount of time you hold each fixation.

It may come as a surprise, but even though you are reading faster than is comfortable, you are still able to grasp meaning. You might not be able to hold on to the meaning for long or connect it to what came before or after, but for that split second, the content does register.

The problem that arises when we read fast is that we can lose control of our eye movements. They can zig-zag violently across the page. As a result, our fixations become messy and careless, causing the eyes to stop on random words and spaces.

Keep that from happening. Try hard to maintain control of the eye jumps and stops. If the eyes are moving too fast to control, slow down until you regain control. As soon as control is regained, play with speeding it back up a bit.

Once you develop control of fixations at a faster pace, read the passage again, but this time, for comprehension. Finally, make sure to practice reducing fixation on the reading materials you gathered.

Now, let's look at the next barrier to speed reading called regression.

Chapter 8 – Regression

Regression lives on, not because of the unavailability of a better option but because of the inertia and fear –EverSkeptic

The last chapter explored fixation and how the eyes pause and fixate on words when reading. This chapter examines regression, which is similar to fixation, but instead of stopping to look at words you are reading, you stop to go back to words you've already read. So, regression is the act of reading the same text multiple times.

Regression is a common behavior, with many readers regularly going back to passages they have already read. They may go back either to pick up missed words or to make sure that their understanding is clear. Whatever the reason, studies show that people spend as much as one third of their time rereading words.

Based on this statistic, it is easy to see why regression is counter-productive. First, as the word implies, reading speed regresses. It is like taking two steps forward and one step back. And when revisiting an entire page or chapter, it's like taking several steps back.

Regression also reduces comprehension. Our minds take meaning from what we just read to help us understand what we are about to read. By skipping back to a previous sentence, paragraph, or section, we can't help but lose track of the point that was being made. So, after regressing, you may have forgotten what you just read, making it difficult to understand what you are about to read.

Most importantly, regression breaks flow, and speed reading is all about flow. It's about syncing the pace of the eyes to the rhythm of the mind. As the eyes see words, the mind processes them. As soon as the mind finishes processing one set of words, the eyes pick up a new set. Like a well-oiled machine, the end of one process triggers the beginning of a new one.

Regression breaks this flow and rhythm, forcing the machine to be re-started. Even worse, by backtracking and regressing often, the mind and eyes never get a chance to get into flow. This severely limits reading potential. Overall, regression doubles, or even triples, reading time and may not even result in better comprehension.

Reasons for Regression

To break this pattern, it helps to understand why we regress in the first place. Some of the reasons are obvious while others are not. Let's look closer at the reasons for regression.

Natural to Regress

Much like fixation, regression is a natural visual process. Just as our eyes constantly fixate and jump when looking at something, they also swing back and forth. They repeatedly move backward, then forward, and then back again.

Watch a person's eyes, without paying attention to any other feature, and you will see just how often their eyes shift back and forth. It's what the eyes do. Those whose eyes move back and forth more often tend to read slower because they regress more frequently.

Lack of Focus

Another cause of regression is lack of concentration. We read but do not pay attention to the text. Our eyes see the words, but the mind is in la-la-land. Since our mind is elsewhere, it therefore doesn't process anything that comes in. As a result, we must revisit the passages where we lost focus.

Subvocalization

Subvocalization can also cause regression for the simple reason that our eyes move faster than our mouths. When the eyes race ahead of the mouth, we must stop and go back to verbally process what we visually saw, thus causing regression.

Wrong Fixation

The most common reason for regression is that our eyes fixate on the wrong spot. As we read, we may lose our place on the page, or we may land our eyes on a spot much further along than we intended. As a result, we must go back and find the right spot.

Habit

As I keep stressing, anything performed long enough becomes a habit. If you regressed when learning to read, that pattern may have internalized as a habit. Now, you regress simply because you've become used to doing it. You don't choose or even want to do it; it just happens simply because your eyes and mind have a habitual *need* to regress.

That's how habits work. They make us do things we have not necessarily chosen to do, want to do, or that is even helpful to do. Habits may even make us think that we missed something important so we go back to a passage.

Avoiding Regression

Understanding the causes of regression puts us in a better position to reduce and stop it. From the explanations, you probably already came up with ways to do that. Let's discuss them now.

Have a Clear Purpose

As explained in Chapter 1, purpose directs attention and focus. With a well-defined purpose, the mind's awareness opens, and its focus changes. It hones in on the task of reading and seeking the precise information you seek. Since the mind is immersed in the content, it does not get lost in thought and miss what is being read, eliminating the need to regress.

Stop Subvocalizing

Since subvocalization can be a culprit in regression, obviously strive to limit it as much as possible. Don't get caught in a dance of trying to match the speed of the mouth with the eyes, tripping yourself up, and having to backtrack.

Index Card

One tried and true method to reduce regression is with the use of an index card. Find an index card the same width of the column you are reading. It is best to use the unlined side of the card.

Begin at the top of the page and slide the card down over each line of text as you read. With the text out of sight, you're unable to look back and regress.

Continue reading and pulling the card down over each line of text that is read until reaching the end of the page. Do the same on the next page. Of course, the urge to peek and remove the index card will arise on occasion, but do the best to resist that urge.

Control Fixations

Although instructed to reduce the number and length of fixations, do so in a controlled manner. Don't be erratic and impulsive with the jumps and stops. Be deliberate in how the eyes move and where they land.

Don't feel pressured to push your reading too hard. Always strive to pick up additional text with each glance and to shorten the time of each glance but not if doing so causes fixations to stop on words you did not intended.

This rule is especially important for beginners. When learning a new skill, beginners hunger to become experts right away. Instead of taking the time to develop their skills, they push through with full steam. Going full steam without developing control causes slips that lead to regression.

Keep in mind, this isn't a contest. Focus on control rather than speed and speed will improve naturally.

Practice Drill

The previous drill added speed to the practice of Space Reading or chunking while reducing subvocalization. In this drill, you will refrain from regressing while doing all this.

As before, begin at the intro and read through the chapter without regressing, even if you miss or feel like you missed something. If it helps, use an index card to cover what has been read so you are not tempted to peek back.

Don't worry if you fail to grasp the content. The point right now is to change the urge to regress. You will learn to comprehend more than you've ever comprehended by pushing yourself to move forward.

By practicing this drill, you'll notice that you regress considerably more than you thought. Much of your regression behavior is outside of your conscious awareness or control. Without realizing, you probably regressed a great deal while applying the drills in earlier chapters. Being conscious of the behavior will help you better overcome it.

At times, the initial urge to regress may be easy to resist, though as you forge ahead, the urge grows stronger. It may grow so strong that it actually becomes a distraction to reading. You won't be able to concentrate because an irritating sensation to revisit a particular section will push you to think something important is being missed. This urge will incessantly annoy you to go back.

On occasion, that urge may be so overpowering that it makes you to lose interest or give up trying to read further. It may argue that there is no use in reading on because whatever was missed will create difficulty in learning what's to come. That logic may kill the drive or enthusiasm to continue reading altogether.

Resist that urge!

Keep plowing forward, even if you feel like you missed something important or don't understand an explanation. Condition your brain that it is not okay to regress, and that you will not regress, no matter how great the temptation. This is how the brain will learn that it must be attentive the first time you read a passage.

Reread this chapter several times while refraining from regression. Then, practice on the other materials.

Ample ground has been covered to take reading to the next level. To round out this section, the next chapter introduces the concept of visual range.

Chapter 9 – Visual Range

Strategic vision is the ability to look ahead and peripheral vision is the ability to look around, and both are important –Carly Fiorina

Speed reading, as we've discussed, is about picking up more words in a single glance or fixation. In order to effectively develop this ability, it's critical to expand your visual range.

Visual range is the ability to see objects beyond your direct line of focus. When looking at something in front of you, it's easy to see that object because the eyes are directly on it. It's difficult to capture details on either side of the object unless you move your eyes.

By expanding your visual range, you can see both what's in front of you and on both sides without the eyes moving. This allows you to capture more words in a single glance.

This requires using peripheral vision, or what you see from the corners of your eyes. Peripheral vision encompasses everything that the eyes can see beyond whatever is directly in front of them. In other words, everything we see from the sides while looking ahead makes up our peripheral. It is the largest part of our visual field.

Peripheral awareness is important because it gives us the ability to react to what's happening around us, not just what's in front. When driving, for example, the peripheral pays attention to the movement of cars to the left and right so that we can focus straight ahead. When walking down a hall, our peripheral stays on guard for anyone who might unexpectedly rush out of a door that we are passing. In both cases, peripheral vision helps us avoid collisions.

We use peripherals more often than you might think. Whenever we try to look at someone without them knowing, we employ peripheral vision. When playing sports such as basketball or football, we engage them to keep track of the players on the field and what they are doing at any given moment.

Although we naturally engage peripheral vision in these activities, we rarely engage it while reading. This is especially true when we've been reading in the same manner for our entire life.

Using peripheral vision is a smart way to enhance reading. In addition to seeing the words directly in front, you can also see words from the corners of the eyes. This naturally widens your visual range so that you can capture more text in a single glance.

Peripheral vision is vital for many reasons beyond widening visual awareness. First, the brain processes information from the sides 25 percent faster than it does from direct vision, which is why the brain is able to react to dangers so quickly.

Engaging the peripheral also softens the eyes' gaze so their focus doesn't narrow down to a single word. Ultimately, using peripheral reduces regression or extended fixations, since one side of the peripheral range can catch words the other side may miss.

If you've never worked on expanding peripheral range, chances are that it isn't very wide. Therefore, the number of extra words it can capture is limited. If that's the case, then in addition to training yourself to use the peripheral while reading, you also want to widen it.

Widening peripheral vision increases the eyes' capacity to capture words from both the left and right corners even further. Developing this is key to developing the skill of speed reading.

Expanding Visual Range

This chapter both trains and widens peripheral field of vision. Through the following six exercises, you will become comfortable using your peripheral while gradually expanding it.

Exercise 1 – Sticks and Straw

For the Sticks and Straw exercise, grab a straw and two toothpicks. Begin by placing the straw horizontally on a desk or table one foot from your eyes. Now, grab one toothpick in each hand, and as you stare at the center of the straw, insert the toothpicks simultaneously into the ends of the straw—one toothpick through each end.

When doing the exercise, look directly at the center of the straw; don't shift the eyes to either the right or the left. Instead, use your peripheral vision to see both ends. Challenge yourself by inserting both toothpicks into the ends of the straw at the same time. Working on one straw end at a time will not stretch peripheral vision.

Exercise 2 – Off the Wall

This exercise requires a ball that fits into one hand, such as a tennis, racket, or bouncy ball. Stand in front of a wall and choose a spot just above eye level. With one hand, bounce the ball off that spot on the wall and catch it with the other hand. Then, bounce it back into the first hand. Repeat this action over and over.

When tossing the ball, don't take your eyes off that spot in front of you. Instead, use your peripheral vision to both throw and catch the ball. That is, look straight ahead as you use peripheral vision to follow the ball leaving one hand and bouncing off the wall to arrive in the other. Be patient as it will take a few repetitions to develop the necessary hand-eye coordination.

If this becomes too easy, take it up a level. Instead of throwing the ball at the wall, throw it over your head from one hand to the other. At a certain point, the ball will leave your peripheral range, which will challenge your peripheral to track the speed of the ball, so it can predict when it will come down.

Exercise 3 – Open Your Awareness

This exercise does not require the use of physical props. Instead, choose a target at eye level where gaze can be comfortably rested. If you are inside, look at the wall or at a picture in front of you. If outside, pick a tree or a street sign in the distance. Wherever you choose to look, hold your gaze and eyes there.

Now, without moving the eyes, gradually begin to notice things to your right and left. Continue to stare at the target while paying careful attention to more and more details in your peripheral range.

This exercise can be done almost anywhere, anytime. For example, while sitting at a desk, gaze directly at the center of the computer screen and take note of everything the peripheries see on and around the desk. If on a bus, choose a point of focus and note the number of people on board, where they are sitting, and what they are wearing, in addition to observing other features of the bus, like windows, seats, and advertisements.

This exercise can even be performed while walking down the street. Use peripheral sight to notice features of buildings and people that you pass.

Exercise 4 – Shultz Table

The Shultz Table is a table or grid, usually with 3x3, 4x4, or 5x5 dimensions, filled with numbers, letters, or words. The goal of the table is to focus attention on the text in the center square while using peripheral vision to identify as many numbers and letters as possible in the outer squares. It is one of the best ways to open visual awareness.

To illustrate, let's use the 3x3 Shultz table below. Fix your gaze on the center square, and then notice the numbers in the surrounding squares. The object is to identify all the numbers in less than one minute.

4	8	9
3	2	6
1	7	5

The 3x3 square might have been too easy, so let's try the 4x4 table below. Since there is no center square, direct your gaze at the center of the table. Then, pick out the first 4 numbers in the inner squares, and then the 12 numbers in the outer squares.

12	8	2	11
7	6	13	16
5	4	10	9
15	3	1	14

The 5x5 table below takes the difficulty up a notch. The same rules apply: identify the 8 numbers around the center square, then move outward to the 16 numbers in the outer square. Again, the object is to identify all the numbers in less than one minute.

20	13	17	18	4
14	15	3	25	21
10	2	9	7	6
24	1	23	19	5
11	12	22	8	16

Employing the Shultz table is a great way to train and expand peripheral vision. Practice using the tables until you can comfortably see the outer numbers with your peripheral.

If you become too familiar with the numbers in the tables provided here, feel free to create your own tables. Simply draw 3x3, 4x4, 5x5, or even 6x6 grids and populate them with random numbers, letters, or words.

Shultz tables can also be found online at the following link: http://www.onedollartips.com/tools/szultz/ Simply type in the number of rows and columns you'd like, and the site will generate a set of custom tables on which to practice.

Exercise 5 – Raining Letters

Below is a table with three columns of letters. Look at the letter in the center column while reciting the letters to the left and right. For example, stare at the letter *S* in the middle of the first row as you try to make out the letters *M* and *N* the sides of the *S*. Then, move down to the next row and look at the letter *X* as you attempt to decipher the letters to its left and right. Continue down each row until the end.

M	S	N
L	X	N
O	H	O
W	U	E
F	L	E
S	E	D
C	A	T
V	L	A
M	U	T
S	A	L
E	E	C
S	I	T
M	N	E
M	N	E
M	U	D
P	I	C
J	H	S
B	O	E

Much like the Shultz table, this first example probably wasn't too challenging, so let's try one with 5 columns. Again, look at the letter in the center column, and move down while reciting the letters in the two columns to the right and left of the center.

O	M	S	N	I
E	L	X	N	I
S	O	H	O	K
A	W	U	E	K
A	F	L	E	L
H	S	E	D	L
O	C	A	T	L
I	V	L	A	L
O	M	U	T	N
T	S	A	L	N
D	E	E	C	N
A	S	I	T	N
I	M	N	E	N
I	M	N	E	N
O	M	U	D	N
R	P	I	C	N
O	J	H	S	N
O	B	O	E	N

If 5 columns weren't challenging enough, the next table takes it up a notch. Remember, the object is to identify all the letters to the immediate left and right of the center column, then continue moving outward to make out the letters in the columns to the far left and right.

S	E	E	EXN	O	S	G
S	C	Z	CTT	U	T	O
P	R	G	RZH	T	E	E
K	E	V	ESH	I	S	R
J	O	H	ORE	C	A	M
H	O	I	ONT	E	S	R
G	U	T	UVH	E	A	I
G	R	S	RAN	I	R	R
G	R	T	RIN	N	O	N
G	I	C	ITE	E	I	A
C	L	T	LOX	N	E	K
C	H	B	HES	I	C	U
C	H	N	HMJ	J	A	I
B	L	D	LRY	N	E	N
A	R	T	RNE	E	C	T
A	L	M	LLN	N	O	O
T	S	W	SNR	E	D	O
S	W	Z	WAR	I	V	L

Exercise 6 – Centered Text

Now that you are comfortable using your peripheral vision, let's begin using it on written material. Below is a poem by W.B. Yeats with a vertical line drawn down the middle. Aim focus on the vertical line, and with your side vision, notice how many words you can make out to the left and right. Move down the vertical line, picking up the words on both sides until you reach the end of the poem.

> The trees are in their autumn beauty, the woodland paths are dry
> Under the October twilight, the water mirrors a still sky
> Upon the brimming water among the stones, are nine and fifty swans
>
> The nineteenth Autumn has come upon me since I first made my count
> I saw, before I had well finished, all suddenly mount
> And scatter wheeling in great broken rings, upon their clamorous wings
>
> I have looked upon those brilliant creatures, and now my heart is sore
> All's changed since I, hearing at twilight, the first time on this shore
> The bell-beat of their wings above my head, trod with a lighter tread
>
> Unwearied still, lover by lover, they paddle in the cold
> Companionable streams or climb the air; their hearts have not grown old
> Passion or conquest, wander where they will, Attend upon them still
>
> But now they drift on the still water; mysterious, beautiful
> Among what rushes will they build, by what lake's edge or pool
> Delight men's eyes, when I awake someday, to find they have flown away

If this is your first attempt at applying peripheral vision toward reading, you might only see one word to the left and right, and likely, they will be blurry. That's okay. Don't let that stop you from continuing down the poem and grabbing what you can.

When you reach the end, go back and do the exercise again. Repeat the exercise regularly and often, stretching your ability to see words on both sides. Once you can clearly see one word on either side of the line, try for two words until they too become clear. Keep working to comfortably see more and more words to the left and right of the center.

With persistence, you will gain the ability to look at the center of a page of any book, article, or essay and quickly make out all the words in an entire row. It will take effort and patience to achieve that level, but it is possible. At this level, you'll be practically *inhaling* information, because all you'll have to do is direct gaze to the middle of a row of text and work down, one row after the next.

You'll notice that this poem is not particularly easy to read or understand, but that's the exact reason it was chosen. The idea is to not become too familiar with the text too soon. When the content becomes familiar, the tendency is to work from memory rather than sight.

Nonetheless, eventually the poem will become familiar enough so you won't need to look as carefully to identify the words to the left and right. Once that happens, apply this exercise to other material. To do so, open a document in a text editor, like Microsoft Word, Google Docs, or Apple Pages. Next, center the paragraphs in the document. Then, as previously instructed, look at the middle of each row, and practice making out as many words to the left and right of the middle as you go down the page.

These 6 exercises offer some powerful ways to train and expand peripheral vision. They are built around the principal of fixing your eyes on a spot in front of you, while opening awareness of the details to the sides.

Be aware, you might unknowingly move your eyes to the left or right to catch a better glimpse. This can happen so quickly, you may not realize that you are doing it, believing that you were looking straight the entire time.

Be cautious of this as you want to capture the side details with peripheral vision, not with direct vision. Otherwise, it defeats the purpose of the exercises.

Also, it helps to use soft focus instead of the hard focus that we commonly use to read. This means relaxing the eyes similar to the way you look at pictures. Soft focus makes better use of peripheral vision. It also puts less strain on the eyes, making it easier to read.

In addition, be sure to do all six of the exercises. People tend to stick to one or two that they like or that are easy, and skip the rest. Few take the time to stick toothpicks into straws or bounce a ball off the wall. They would much rather sit in front of their computer working the Shultz table.

Although any one of these exercises is helpful on its own, the benefits compound by doing them all. Practicing one exercise will improve your ability with another, so make it a point to run through all 6. Each one takes a few seconds to a few minutes to complete, so the time commitment is minimal, yet the benefits gained are vast.

Practice Drill

Before starting any drills, run through the exercises several times to get comfortable using and expanding peripheral vision. The drill will have more impact after going a few rounds with the 6 exercises outlined in this chapter.

As your visual range begins expanding, apply it to a reread of this chapter. Combining instructions from previous chapters and drills, read this chapter with wider visual awareness. Try to catch one additional word to the left and right beyond your current ability.

Until now, you've been asked to space read or chunk every 3 to 4 words. Attempt reading this chapter picking up 4 to 5 words in between every space or chunk. Continue the practice on the other materials.

Once Space Reading or chunking every 4 to 5 words while limiting subvocalization, fixation, and regression is in reach, advance to 5 to 6 words. After reaching that level, move up to 6 to 7 words and on up.

Though bear in mind that moving up in levels takes time, effort, persistence, and practice. No reader can progress that quickly in a single sitting. You'll need to practice widening peripheral, then practice the drills, then go back to the exercises to widen peripheral further, then back to the drills again over an extended period.

This concludes section III on enhancing the techniques. Remember, fixation and regression are enemies of speed reading, and visual range a friend. Now, let's look at how to better understand written material.

Before moving to the next section, I want to say I get plagiarized a lot

And I mean, a lot!

There are countless books on Amazon alone that have copied my work, sometimes word for word.

Don't believe me? Check out these reviews:

www.amazon.com/gp/customer-reviews/R23VFGCXBF35K6/

www.amazon.com/gp/customer-reviews/R2HQBPE9XMCUG4/

www.audible.com/listener/AVD2ZZTASWWPK

If that wasn't bad enough...

These copiers post malicious negative reviews on my book to boost their own sales.

It takes time and effort to address each issue, and often it doesn't get resolved.

If it does, somebody else comes along with another copy.

I found the only way to deal with this issue is to continue building reviews.

Therefore, if you like what you have read so far, please take a moment to leave a review

It takes only a few seconds and only need be a few words, but it will help protect the hard work or original authors and keep the book industry from becoming a plagiarized mess.

To leave a review, simply:

1. Click this link
2. Scroll down to the reviews and click [Write a review]
3. Write a few words

Doing so will allow me to keep writing great content for you, protect legitimate authors, and safe guard the industry :)

Section IV – Improving Comprehension

Chapter 10 – Reading for Ideas or Main Points

Great minds discuss ideas; average minds discuss events –Eleanor Roosevelt

As noted in the intro, speed reading is not reading without comprehension. Otherwise, you are merely looking at words really fast. This is the reason this book dedicates an entire section solely to comprehension and grasping the meaning, message, and content of the material you read.

The first step to comprehension is seeking out the main points. When reading, it is critical to pay attention to the main idea or overarching point the writer is trying to communicate. That is, it's one thing to make sense of a single sentence or paragraph but a whole other to grasp the overall message of a passage.

Paying attention only to details, such as facts, dates, and descriptions, without giving thought to the main points, can lead to missing crucial information essential for understanding and memory. While studying history, for example, you might read about events and be oblivious to the country or person to whom they relate. Or, you might read instructions without grasping the bigger picture of what they will help you do.

To illustrate, if you asked a friend how their weekend went, how would you like him or her to respond? Would you prefer to hear, *I went on vacation?* Or would you prefer, *I pulled out my luggage, packed it with clothes, zipped it up, drove to the airport, checked in my bags, flew to Mexico, took a taxi to a hotel, and sat in front of a beach drinking mojitos?*

This is how people read. They pay attention to the details, but not the main points. They pick up the packing, driving, and flying without understanding it is for vacation. The main point is *vacation* , the rest are *details* . If you don't grasp the main point, you will get lost in the details.

To illustrate further, think back to Chapter 7, which discussed the eyes' need to stop and fixate in order to focus. This was explained not to show off about the amazing features of the eyes but instead to illustrate the effect of fixation on reading speed and comprehension. The *main point* of the chapter was to explain how reducing the number and duration of fixations can improve reading.

If you failed to catch how the *detail* of fixation affects the *big picture* of reading speed, you would miss the fundamental lesson of the chapter. You might know what fixation is and why it is important to vision, and even be fascinated by how often the eyes jump and pause, but that knowledge won't help improve reading.

Again, this is how most people read, especially students. They notice the details but miss the **bigger context or point** . As a result, they get lost and don't understand what they've read.

To improve comprehension, pay attention to the main points or the big picture, so to speak, and the broader context. When sifting through a lot of details, take an occasional step back to identify how those details relate to the overall message the author is trying to communicate.

Most books, especially academic ones, are written with main points in mind, so it should not be difficult to identify them. Sometimes, it's as simple as asking, *what is the point of this sentence, paragraph, or passage* ?

This is not to imply that main points are more important than details—both matter. If a friend says he went on vacation, you naturally want to know more. On the other hand, if they simply recite a bunch of activities without explaining that it was for a vacation, you'd either be really confused or think they lost their minds.

A good way to recognize the main points is to recognize the levels embedded in any written composition. It begins with understanding the meaning of a sentence, then how that sentence fits into the paragraph, and then how the paragraph supports the larger chapter. Finally, how the chapter supports the overall piece.

A writer doesn't pick random words to form sentences, then casually combine those sentences into paragraphs, and haphazardly order the paragraphs into chapters. Enormous work and intention go into the craft of writing to give the final work structure and coherence. Just as there is a purpose to why we read, there is a purpose to why writers write. To drive the point home, there is a point that a writer is trying to make, and it is your job as readers to understand that point.

You may think you understand the point of a passage, but unless you are actively seeking it, you will likely miss it. So always be on the hunt for the bigger meaning, idea, or purpose. Don't get caught in only the details.

The process can also be applied in reverse. Since the preview step gives you a general overview of a written piece, determine the overall message or point of the material during preview. Then, while reading, watch for how the author delivers and supports that message with the details. Think about the ways each chapter supports the overall book, how the individual paragraphs reinforce each chapter, and how specific sentences develop the paragraphs.

For example, the overall point of this book is to teach simple techniques to improve reading speed. Each chapter presents a specific technique that helps readers with that goal. The techniques are defined, explained, and illustrated within the subsections and paragraphs of the chapter.

Looking at chapter 8 on regression, the first subsection defines regression and its impact on reading, the second explains the causes of regression, and the third offers advice on how to overcome them. Diving further, each paragraph presents an argument, a cause, and a solution. Within the paragraph, each sentence supports the point the paragraph is making.

The more ideas you can identity and the more you can figure out how the details support those ideas, the easier it will be to comprehend the material fully. You will evolve from merely reading words and sentences to grasping whole concepts and positions. Comprehension will advance beyond facts and dates to truly understanding what is being communicated in the material and why.

Practice Drill

Think back to the introduction and the last 9 chapters of this book, and reflect on the main points discussed in each chapter and how the details supported the points.

There's no need to do this from memory—just yet. Revisit the chapters and review the content. In addition, scan the table of contents to get a better sense of the structure and organization of each chapter.

Think about what each chapter is trying to communicate and why. Although the chapter titles give away the main point, go beyond restating the title, and describe the underlying message. For example, as the title of chapter 2 suggests, the main point is *preview*. What is preview, and why is it important?

Each chapter also offers an assortment of details, such as examples, illustrations, stories, instructions, and exercises to support the main points. Think about what these details aspire to communicate. They are not there by accident.

For example, what was the point of the lengthy explanation in Chapter 2 of why humans make mistakes or the story of my friend in Belize? Those stories weren't for entertainment. How did they support the overall topic of *preview*?

Again, if you focus only on the *details* of the story, you might miss the underlying purpose or argument. We all fall into this trap. It is easy to be captivated by a fascinating fact and settle on that as the main point.

After reviewing the chapters in this book, find the main points in the sample materials. If you've been doing the drills in the previous chapters, you should have read them multiple times by now. Think about what the writer of each piece wishes to share.

The concept of mining for the main point transitions nicely into the next chapter, which discusses the structure of a paragraph. This valuable knowledge will increase the speed with which you grasp meaning and intent in anything you read.

Chapter 11 – Topic Sentences

If a thesis is a road map to a paper, then a topic sentence is a guide to a paragraph –BCCC Tutoring Center

The previous chapter taught the importance of identifying the main points or ideas when reading. It also provided two ways to identify those points. This chapter will provide another way to do that, which involves recognizing the principal thought or purpose of a paragraph.

As you know, a paragraph is a group of sentences that discusses one idea. The idea can describe a place, detail a character, illustrate a process, or reveal information about an event. It can also argue or explain a point or help develop an argument or point.

Paragraphs are the fundamental units of all writing because they are the building blocks, much like bricks to a house, which hold together a piece of writing. An idea in one paragraph leads to an idea in the next, and so on, until the reader comes to understand the big picture the writer is trying to convey.

Since each paragraph discusses a distinct idea, as readers, our task is to locate that idea in each paragraph. The way to do this is to identify the **topic sentence** —the sentence that clearly states the idea. To understand what a topic sentence is and how to find it, it helps to understand the formal structure of a paragraph.

Structure of Paragraph

In formal writing, paragraphs consist of three parts: *topic sentence* , *supporting sentences* , and *concluding sentence* .

Topic Sentence

As mentioned, the topic sentence presents the paragraph's main idea. It acts as the introduction that tells the reader what the rest of the paragraph will be about. The topic sentence also holds facts and details together. When a writer presents a series of facts or descriptions on the same idea, those facts are grouped together and summarized with a topic sentence.

Supporting Sentences

As the name suggests, supporting sentences *support* the topic sentence. They are the details that describe, illustrate, communicate, or explain the topic sentence using facts, reasons, examples, definitions, comparisons, and other pertinent info. Supporting sentences sell the idea made by the topic sentence.

Concluding Sentence

The concluding sentence brings the paragraph to a close. It does this either by restating the topic sentence or by summarizing the information presented in the supporting sentences. Since the concluding sentence restates and summarizes previous information, it is similar to, but not exactly the same as, the topic sentence. These sentences often lead the reader into the next paragraph.

In many ways, paragraphs resemble hamburgers. The top bun is the topic sentence, the bottom bun concluding sentence, and the meat and trimmings supporting sentences. Although the top and bottom buns look similar, they are not exactly the same. Nonetheless, both buns hold the core of the burger together in the same way that topic and concluding sentences hold together supporting sentences in a paragraph. Such is the nature of paragraphs.

Let's use the previous paragraph to illustrate. The first sentence, *In many ways, paragraphs resemble hamburgers*, is the topic sentence, setting the stage for what will be discussed, which is how paragraphs resemble hamburgers. The next three sentences support and expand upon the relationship between paragraphs and hamburgers. The last sentence, *Such is the nature of paragraphs*, summarizes the main point while also concluding the paragraph.

This is the formal structure that teachers taught us, if we were so inclined to pay attention. The format is used in a wide variety of written materials, such as books, articles, magazines, essays, and journals. The format is particularly popular in academic and non-fiction works.

Your goal is to find the topic sentence in each paragraph and understand how the other sentences detail, elaborate, or describe the claim the topic sentence makes. This practice yields greater insight into how the paragraph fits into the overall piece.

Finding the Topic Sentence

So how do you find the topic sentence? While it may appear anywhere in the paragraph, it is most often the first sentence, because it introduces what follows. Reviewing the topic sentence in the previous example, *In many ways, paragraphs resemble hamburgers*, you'll notice it is the first sentence. In fact, majority of the topic sentences in this book are the first sentence of their respective paragraph.

Also, topic sentences tend to be short and general with limited content. That is because they use supporting sentences to provide the necessary details. By reviewing the topic sentences in this book, you will notice that they are general and relatively shorter than the other sentences.

Topic sentences often pose a question to be answered. The statement, *In many ways, paragraphs resemble hamburgers,* raises the questions: *Why are they like hamburgers*? Or, *How do they resemble hamburgers*? This makes a reader want to dive into the supporting sentences for answers. If unsure whether or not a sentence is the topic, try turning it into a question. If the other sentences seem to answer that question, then you have identified the topic sentence.

Sometimes, you can spot the topic sentence by finding a word or two that repeat in the rest of the paragraph. In the previous paragraph, the topic sentence is, *Another way to identify a topic sentence is that it often poses a question to be answered*. We can safely assume this is the topic sentence because a) it is the first and most general sentence in the paragraph, and b) one of the words in the sentence, *question*, shows up 2 additional times. This i a good indication that this sentence is likely the topic sentence.

Furthermore, topic sentences often contain transition words that smoothly lead the reader from one paragraph to the next. These include words that show continuity, like *next* , *another* , *also* , *in addition* , or words that express disagreement, like *despite* , *nevertheless* , *however* , and *although* . I'm a big f of transition words as they really help refine the flow of my writing. A quick glance at the previous 5 paragraphs and you'll notice many of them use transition words. Not surprisingly, those sentences are also the topic sentences of the paragraph.

Lastly, it's not uncommon to find topic sentences following a transition sentence. Transition sentences, like transition words, bridge the end of one paragraph to the beginning of the next. They are always the first sentence of a new paragraph, so you are likely to find the topic sentence immediately following them.

Let's revisit the following paragraph that appeared earlier in this chapter:

> So, how do you find the topic sentence? While it may appear anywhere in the paragraph, it is most often the first sentence, because it introduces what follows. Reviewing the topic sentence in the previous example, *Think of paragraphs like hamburgers* , you'll notice it is the first sentence. In fact, a majority of the topic sentences in this book are the first sentence in the paragraph.

Although the first sentence in this paragraph may seem like a topic sentence, it is merely a transition sentence that smoothly transitions the reader from the previous paragraph.

The sentence that follows is the true topic of the paragraph as it introduces the main thought. And if you notice, it has the word *first* , which shows up several times throughout the passage. This increases the likelihood that the sentence is the topic. You don't see the words in the transition sentence, like *find* , repeated in the passage.

Although the topic sentence is often the first sentence in a paragraph, it can show up elsewhere. It can appear as the second, third, and occasionally, even as the final. When it comes last, the supporting sentences are used to develop arguments and examples that build to the main idea announced at the end.

Again, your goal when reading is to be on the hunt for the topic sentence. It will help you understand the thought or idea of a paragraph. Although a thought or idea of a paragraph is not the main or overarching point of a composition, it will allow you follow the writers line of thinking form one paragraph to the next to get to the main or overarching point of a composition. Topic sentences are what keep the conversation going from one paragraph to the next.

Practice Drill

This drill will test your ability to find topic sentences. Identify which sentence is the topic sentence in the following paragraphs taken from http://www.laflemm.com:

> *The 1920s began on a note of economic optimism. However, by the end of the decade, America was sinking into an economic depression that left the country reeling. Automobile sales, the heart of the early twenties consumer boom, were bottoming out. Housing starts fell, along with manufacturing output. In the fall of 1929, the stock market crashed with investors losing as much money as the government had spent during all of World War I. Those without investments on Wall Street were facing even grimmer prospects. Jobs were disappearing as factories and businesses closed their doors. For many working people, it wasn't clear if they would have a roof over their head or enough food to feed themselves and their families.*

Although the first sentence seems like it could be the topic sentence, it is only a transition sentence that paves the way for sentence 2, the true topic. Sentence 1 discusses the high point of the early twenties, but that discussion doesn't continue on the high point.

Sentence 2 talks about the *country reeling*, and that reeling is described in the remaining sentences. The second sentence also uses the phrase *economic depression*, and although the other sentences don't repeat those specific words, they use similar ones, such as *bottoming out*, *fell*, *crashed*, and *losing* words associated with economic depression. You may also have noticed that the second sentence begins with the transition word *however*. Given all this, it's safe to assume that this is the topic of the paragraph.

Let's examine another example. Read the following paragraph and find the topic sentence.

> The rules of conduct during an examination are clear. No books, calculators or papers are allowed in the test room. Proctors will not allow anyone with such items to take the test. Anyone caught cheating will be asked to leave the room. His or her test sheet will be taken. The incident will be reported to the proper authority. At the end of the test period, all materials will be returned to the proctor. Failure to abide by these rules will result in a failing grade for this test.

The first sentence is the topic of the paragraph. Although no major words from the first sentence are repeated, we do see variations of the word *examination* or words that are related to exams, such as *test*, *cheating*, *test sh* and *proctor*. The conclusion effectively restates the first sentence and summarizes the paragraph about following the rules.

Let's look at one final example. This one is longer and more difficult.

> Whenever a dictionary gets revised, the editors have to select those words worthy of making its pages. Sometimes that decision is difficult because it's just not clear which words have entered the English language long-term and which ones reflect momentary fads that will be gone in a year or two, along with the words that described them. The following words, though, don't fall into that "iffy" category; they seem to be keepers, deserving of an entry in any comprehensive, or complete, dictionary. The word "telenovelas," for instance, refers to the Spanish version of

soap operas. Given the popularity of this particular entertainment form, room for it will have to made in the T section of every desk dictionary. The same is true for "Bollywood," the name given to movies made in Bombay, India and modeled on old Hollywood films that were heavy on passionate romance, singable tunes, and superficial plot lines. It's also hard to believe that references to I-pods are going to disappear anytime soon; so "IPO," initial public offering and "Ipoh," a city in Malaysia, should get ready to make space for a new entry. It's also probably true, too, that the word "gninormous," meaning "huge" or "gigantic," is not just a flash in the pan. Thus, it's very likely to turn up in updated dictionaries, probably accompanied by "technostalgia" (a longing for simpler forms of technology that have been replaced)

If you picked the first sentence as the topic, you are incorrect. If you chose the second sentence, you are also incorrect. I mentioned this example was difficult. The topic is in sentence three. Sentence three introduces words deserving of entry into the dictionary, something the rest of the paragraph lists. Also, the word *keeper* vibrates throughout the text.

Don't be discouraged if the last example proved challenging. It takes time and practice, but eventually, you will be able to spot the topic sentence in the first read without a second thought.

Continue practicing with the passages in the other materials. Pick out the topic sentence in each paragraph.

Chapter 12 – Vocabulary

As vocabulary is reduced, so are the number of feelings you can express, the number of events you can describe, the number of the things you can identify
–Sheri S. Tepper

To truly ameliorate the dexterity to subsume written material, one must possess a wieldy argot. Without a philistine vernacular, it's perverse to elucidate any prose. You would be quixotic to speed read without the aptitude to antithesize the words. Otherwise, it will create a gnawing sense of ennui.

The previous paragraph probably didn't make much sense. It contains big words that make reading and understanding a challenge. As a result, it slowed your reading and was likely draining to get through, depleting any motivation to continue.

This exercise was meant to illustrate the importance of vocabulary on reading speed. As you noticed, not knowing the definition of a word dramatically slows reading. Our eyes fixate on unfamiliar words longer, and there is a greater impulse to regress. You're not aware of it, but you can't help but read slower.

A strong vocabulary is essential to increasing reading speed. Studies show that people with a strong vocabulary not only understand more but read faster. The stronger the vocabulary, the more words the brain can recognize and process in the moment. This helps us pick up meaning quickly, and the quicker we pick up meaning, the quicker we read.

Unfortunately, building vocabulary is not easy. Unlike the previous techniques, this is not one that can be cultivated in a few weeks or even months. It takes time and effort to expand verbal repertoire (a list or supply of skills). The process can even be boring and tedious, causing one to skip developing this skill altogether.

Though, this is a critical area that should not be skipped.

Speed reading will not work with a weak vocabulary. A weak vocabulary increases fixation, regression, and disrupts pace and rhythm. Truth be told, it's almost pointless to speed through text with opaque (difficult to understand) words, because even though you could be read fast, you wouldn't understand their meaning. It helps to have the basics down first, and that includes vocabulary.

Most people shriek (cry or shout) at the thought of improving their vocabulary, thinking that it would be boring or time consuming, not to mention difficult. Many throw in the towel on speed reading, especially those who don't have a strong command of the English language, simply because they feel this is too large a hurdle to overcome.

Building Vocabulary

Traditional methods of building vocabulary, which involve memorizing words in a dictionary, can be boring, time consuming, and challenging. Fortunately, this chapter doesn't take that traditional approach. Rather, it presents unique and creative ways that take little time and effort to follow. Rather than memorize a dictionary, these techniques expose one to more words in day-to-day life while naturally engaging the brain to pick up their meaning and context.

Circle Unfamiliar Words

A great place to start is with material you are already reading. When you stumble on words that are unfamiliar, circle them and move on. Once the passage is finished, return to the circled words, and look up their definition. Then, reread the sentence or paragraph with the new definition in mind. Notice how the sentence or paragraph is clearer now that you know its meaning. This system deepens vocabulary without needing to stop mid-sentence to look up words.

Use a Thesaurus

Use both a dictionary and thesaurus when looking up the meaning of words. Although dictionaries provide the definition, a thesaurus offers synonyms, or alternative words with similar meanings. Synonyms not only raise your ability to understand a word but expose you to more words. This way, the meaning of several words is learned at the same time. For example, if you look up the word *replete* and see that *brimming*, *rife*, and *awash* share a simil definition, you've added three additional words to your vocabulary.

Read a Variety of Materials

Different materials use different types of words. For example, science fiction and fantasy books use a lot of imagery words. Romance novels employ words that are descriptive. Words used in academic texts are specific, while how-to books use general language. Fashion and gossip magazines continually change and evolve expressions. Reading a variety of materials exposes the mind to a wider range of words in meaningful contexts.

Listen to Audiobooks

Audiobooks are a great way to learn the meaning of words. The brain understands words not only based on what is said but on *how* it is said. When word is spoken, auditory cues such as tone, manner, and accent aid the mind in grasping its meaning. Remember, language was at first entirely verbal. The mind evolved to comprehend spoken words before written words.

Another benefit of audiobooks over traditional books is that you can listen to audiobooks while doing other things, like driving, exercising, or lying in bed. All you need to do is press play and go about your business. This means you can go through more books than otherwise—and more books means exposure to more words.

Learn Prefixes and Suffixes

A prefix is a letter or combination of letters added to the beginning of a word to create a new word with a different meaning. For example, adding the prefix *un* to the word *happy* creates the word *unhappy*, which has the opposit meaning of the original word. Adding *over* to *work* creates the new word *overwork*. Ironically, the term prefix uses a prefix itself, as *pre* (which means before) is joined to the word *fix* (which means to attach), creating a word that means *attach before*. This perfectly describes its function of attaching letters before a word.

A suffix, on the other hand, is a letter combination added to the end of a word, like *ish* to *child* to form *childish* or *er* to *work* to form *worker*. Often, the suffix won't change the meaning of the word but will alter its function, as when *ly* is added to the word *quick* to form *quickly* or *ness* to *dark* to form *dar*

Learning the meanings of some of the common prefixes and suffixes will hint at the definition of words that use them. Spending a little time learning a small list of terms goes a long way toward learning and understanding a larger quantity of words.

As the chapter on preview eluded, the mind loves to make predictions and is always on the hunt to figure out what something means or to guess what's going to happen. Prefixes and suffixes help our minds make better predictions. If an unfamiliar word is presented in the correct context, the mind can use the prefix or suffix to accurately guess the meaning without having to pull out a dictionary.

The following two tables list prefixes and suffixes commonly used in the English language. Study and ingrain these terms, and notice how they show up in the words you read.

Prefix	Definition	Example
acro-	high, top	**acrobat** - someone who performs difficult jumping **acrophobia** - fear of heights or high places
amphi-	two, both, or both sides	**amphibians** - animals that live both on land and in water **amphicentric** - centering at both ends
bi-	two	**biannual** - twice a year **bicycle** - cycle with two wheels **bifocal** - eyeglass lenses with two focal lengths
bio-	life	**biology** - study of life **biography** - written account of a person's life
centi-	one hundred or hundredth	**centigrade** - temperature scale going from 0 to 100 **centimeter** - unit of length measuring 100th of a meter **centipede** - worm like arthropods with 100 legs
circum-	around, surround, all sides	**circumstance** - condition surrounding an event or action **circumvent** - to get around, go around, or bypass **circumnavigate** - sail or fly all the away around
di-	two, twice, double	**dichotomy** – division into two opposing parts **diatomic** – molecules with two atoms **dilemma** – difficult choice between two or more options
dys-	abnormal, impaired, difficult	**dysfunctional** – not operating correctly **dyslexia** – learning disorder that involves reading **dystopia** – a bad or unpleasent place or state
ex-	out of, from	**excerpt** - a passage chosen from a specific work **exhale** – breathe out **exit** – a way out
hemi-	half	**hemisphere** - half of a sphere **hemitrope** – half inverted **hemistich** – half of a line of verse
hypo-	below, under, beneath	**hypodermic** – the region right beneath the skin **hypoxia** – deficiency of oxygen reaching tissue **hypoglycemia** – low blood sugar level
im-	not	**immobile** - motionless, not moving **impossible** – not possible **impolite** – not polite
inter-	among, between, during	**intercommunal** – existing between communities **interconnected** – connected with one another **international** – between nations
juxta-	alongside, near	**juxtapose** – place side by side for contrast **juxtapyloric** – near the pylorus **juxtaintestinal** – near the intestines
mono-	one, single	**monolingual** – speaking only one language **monotheism** – religion that believes in one god **monologue** – speech by a single actor
olig-	small, few, little	**oligarch** – small group that control or run a government **oligopoly** – market with little or limited competition **oliguria** – production of abnormally small amt of urine

For a list of more prefixes, please visit: mindlily.com/speedreadingprefix

Suffix	Definition	Example
-able	capable of doing or being the thing indicated by the prefix or stem	**understandable** - able to be understood
		quantifiable - capable of measuring or quantifying
		controllable - cabpable of controlling
-ac	affected by, pertaining to	**pyromaniac** - cumpulsion to set things on fire
		insomniac - person regularly unable to sleep
		brainiac - an exceptionally intelligent person
-agogue	to drive, to make flow	**galactagogue** - a food or drug that increases lactation
		ptyalagogue - Promoting the flow of saliva
		secretagogue - a substance that promotes secretion
-aceous	composed of, full of, partaking of	**curvaceous** - having an attractive curved shape
		predaceous - living by seizing or taking prey
		herbaceous - of, denoting, or relating to herbs
-cide	chop, kill, murder	**genocide** - systematic killing of a nation, race or group
		insecticide - substance used to kill insects
		fungicide - chemical that destroys fungus
-duct	vessel, tube	**oviduct** - fallopian tubes
		aqueduct - an artificial channel for transporting water
		viaduct - bridge carrying a road or railroad over a valley
-el/elle/ella	small, little one	**novella** - story that is shorter than a novel
		morsel - a small piece of food; bite
		fontanelle - space between bone of skull in infant
-ian	relating to, native of, like	**Algerian** - a native or inhabitant of Algeria
		saurian - a lizard like reptile
		logician - person who studies or is skilled in logic
-ess	indicates the female gender	**goddess** - female god or diety
		lioness - female lion
		temptress - woman who lures or tempts a person
-esthetic	pertaining to sensation	**paresthetic** - sensation of pricking, tingling, or creeping
		kinesthetic - learning through touch
		aesthetic - concerned with look or beauty
-fer	someone or something that carries, bears, or produces the thing indicated by the stem	**waterproofer** - make something impenetrable to water
		Roofer - person who constructs or repairs roofs
		Conifer - tree that bears cones and evergreen leaves
-graphy	relating to writing or written	**stenography** - art of writing in shorthand
		calligraphy - artistic or stylized handwriting or lettering
		typography - arranging written material for printing
-ia	pathological state; specified condition of a disease or process	**hyperesthesia** - excessive physical sensitivity
		hyperglycemia - excess of glucose in the bloodstream
		hypochondria - abnormal anxiety about one's health
-less	lacking, free from, without	**fearless** - lacking anxiety
		joyless - grim or dismal
		childless - not having any kids

For a list of more suffixes, please visit: mindlily.com/speedreadingsuffix

Talk to People with Strong Vocabulary

As recently mentioned, language is, first and foremost, verbal. We learned to speak before we learned to read or write. So, nothing connects terms and definitions directly to the brain like talking to people.

This technique only works, of course, when talking to people whose vocabulary is strong. Speaking only to people with a weak vocabulary will not produce the desired results.

Most of us know people who are eloquent speakers—those who have a knack for injecting the right word at the right time to accurately convey a thought, feeling, or situation. If you don't know people like that, seek them out.

Many circumlocute (avoid or withdraw) from such people, either because we don't feel smart enough or we prejudge them as arrogant. Avoiding them, unfortunately, will not help grow vocabulary. Don't feel shy or embarrassed to ask people to define unfamiliar words they use in conversation.

An easy approach is to ask: *What do you mean by . . . ?* Or, *What do you mean when you say . . . ?* For example, if they use the word *replete*, you can ask, *What do you mean by replete?* Or, *What do you mean when you say replete?* Asking a question this way doesn't reveal that you are unaware of a word's meaning—it simply signals that you seek clarification.

Though, it's unnecessary to use such a roundabout approach. It is fine to ask a person directly for a word's meaning. Most people won't embarrass or make you feel dumb for seeking a definition. In my experience, people respect those who show enough care about what they are saying to seek clarification.

After learning a word, practice using it in conversations with other people. This will reinforce memory and understanding of the word. Don't be surprised if others begin asking *you* to define the words you're using!

Study More Words

Finally, a tried and true method to expand vocabulary is simply to study more words. This doesn't mean mindlessly memorizing the dictionary, though if that's your thing, go for it! There are a variety of alternate and fun ways to study vocabulary using apps, software, games, and even online videos. These options allow one to learn faster and more thoroughly than would a mere dictionary.

These are some creative ways to grow your lexicon (the vocabulary of a person, language, or branch of knowledge). This is definitely a long-term approach to improving reading speed. As stated, don't expect results in hours, days, or even weeks. Frequent and consistent effort must be applied over several months to reap the benefits.

Although this skill takes work, it is worth the time and effort. Just 3 months growing vocabulary will yield a lifetime of benefits. Not only will this accelerate reading but the ability to understand more people and more things, thus increasing your overall intelligence.

People often assume their vocabulary will develop simply by reading more, or by reading more challenging literature. Relying solely on reading to build vocabulary is a passive approach that is not very effective. It's a shortsighted view that limits potential. To develop vocabulary, you must actively work on it.

Practice Drill

Apply the tips outlined in this chapter to the sample materials. Read through a piece and circle unfamiliar words. After reviewing the samples, look up definitions of circled words with both a dictionary and thesaurus. Then, practice using these words in everyday conversation.

This completes the section on improving comprehension of written material. To recap, reading for main points, identifying topic sentences, and building vocabulary are the three keys to unlocking the capacity to learn. If you are going to put in the time to read, make sure to do it right.

Let's now proceed to the chapters in the final section.

Section V – Additional Tips

Chapter 13 – Remembering What You Read

Some people are born with wonderful memories and have no trouble keeping things straight. Those born without this incredible ability have to find ways to strengthen their memories –Jane Peters

When I was in Brazil a few years ago, I met an interesting woman who loved books. I mean, she really loved books. So much so that she was always reading. And I mean *always* reading.

She didn't have a steady job or regular work schedule. In the evenings, she was a hostess at a restaurant, and during the day, a tour guide but only when she had tourists to guide. In between, she picked up odd jobs.

In between that, she was reading. Even at work, she was reading. As a hostess, one of her duties was to invite tourists walking by the restaurant in for a meal. If there was a lull in traffic, even for a minute, she would turn to the book she hid in the corner.

Since then, I've met others who are as passionate about reading. They'll read just about any type of material, from books and magazines to newspapers and novels.

One thing I notice about these people is that although they are well read, they often don't remember much of what they've read. Sure, they remember it in the moment, or perhaps for a few days, but not for much longer than that. They simply forget majority of the content.

In my memory improvement material, I teach students not to rely on their automatic mental processes to remember information. Believe it or not, we forget up to 80 percent of what we hear, see, or learn within a few hours of hearing, seeing, or learning it!

This applies to reading as well.

If no attempt is made to remember material, the brain will not retain it. You'll have a sense that you do in fact remember, but as soon as you try to recall that information, you'll realize that in actuality, you can't.

This applies to all types of content, whether fiction or non-fiction, a lengthy book or short article. It also applies to all types of readers, whether a college professor or department store cashier, a newbie, or like my Brazilian friend, a book worm.

Our minds cannot possibly record everything that enters its awareness. A great deal must be discarded, including much of the material that we read.

Suffice to say, if you are going to put in the effort to read something, you probably want to remember it. It is pointless to spend so much time learning to speed read if at the end of the day 80 percent is forgotten.

So, in addition to reading a passage, take action to reinforce your memory of it. When we read non-stop, our brain automatically replaces the old information with the new. By the time we reach the end, we likely have forgotten much of the beginning or middle.

Recall and Review

The way to prevent forgetting is to do what I term *Recall and Review*. While reading, stop at some point and recall what you just read or learned up to that point. You can stop either every half hour or so, or stop every chapter, lesson, or subsection.

It is important that the content is recalled from memory rather than looking at notes or going back to the material. Allow the information to come to mind on its own without looking at anything else.

When confident that you've recalled everything, revisit the passage or any notes you took to see if what you remembered was accurate and complete. It can help to underline important areas while reading, then go back to review those areas.

Adding this process of review after recall ensures that you remembered everything correctly and that it remains fresh. It's a simple step that takes very little time but can have a significant impact on reading and memory.

The fact is if you don't actively do something to remember what you read, you're going to lose it. It's not a question of if, but when, and that *when* is usually within hours.

A great time to practice recall and review is during breaks. After returning from break, quickly recall what you read so far, before moving ahead. For example, if you read two chapters of a novel during the morning commute, the next time you pick up the novel, take a minute to review what you read that morning before reading further. This will not only refresh memory of the previous material but segue smoothly into the new content.

Recall and review is especially useful at the end. After finishing a book, article, or other piece of writing, take a moment to reflect on everything. Try to recall as much as possible, and when you can't recall anything further, quickly review the material to ensure that what you remember is accurate and complete. This will cement the information in memory.

Now let's discuss what to focus on during the recall and review. If reading a story or novel, think about the events that occurred in the story since you last read—what happened to the characters and what did their dialogue reveal? Were new characters introduced, did old ones leave, or were there major twists or turns in the plot? See if you can recall scenery or elements of scenes that were important to the story or that stood out.

With non-fiction, use the suggestions in the previous section and target main points and topic sentences. Can you recall the key points the author made? What details did the author provide to support his or her claim? Think about any information that was fascinating, though don't assume that because a fact is fascinating that you will automatically remember it. Also, keep in mind that what you found so captivating may not be the main point!

When you first attempt this exercise, you may not be able to recall much.

You were attentive and engaged while reading because you understood the material, but now you're drawing a blank. It's as if the brain held the content only long enough to understand the next sentence or paragraph before throwing it out.

If this describes your experience, then you, in fact, understand the mind discards 80 percent of what is read, sometimes within minutes or even seconds of reading it. That's why the recall and review exercise is so vital.

In fact, this technique actually trains the mind to hold on to more of what it reads. If the mind knows that it will be called upon to remember a passage, it will work harder to remember it. Since it knows the information will be used later, it will think twice before throwing it all out.

In effect, recall promotes concentration. It's a natural byproduct of the exercise. Suddenly, you begin paying more attention to the content because the mind is aware it will need to recite the content later. All you need to do is develop the habit of regularly recalling and reviewing written material and concentration will improve naturally.

If a book takes a week to finish, and throughout the week, you take a few moments to regularly recall the material, your memory and comprehension will be far greater than if you read the book twice or even three times. Information won't disappear like it does for so many others.

As with purpose and preview, most prefer to skip this step. They would much rather jump to the next reading or assignment than spend time to recall and review what they just read.

You too might be inclined to skip this step, but understand that this advice is meant to foster memory and comprehension, not to force you to do things you dislike. To improve memory, learning, and comprehension, add this valuable step of recall and review.

Practice Drill

Recall what you read in this chapter beginning with something easy, like the main point or title of the chapter.

Next, can you recall how the chapter started? Yes, it started with a story about a woman I met. Do you remember where we met? What about the story I told about her? Right, she loved books. How did I use that story to lead into the discussion of this chapter?

What else can you remember? Do you remember why recall and review is important? How much of what we read, hear, and see do we lose within an hour? Were specific instructions offered in this chapter? If so, what were they?

Once you have tried to recall as much as possible, review the chapter to see if what you remembered is accurate and complete. If this is your first attempt at mental recall, you will probably miss many points. Even veterans of this technique miss something. That's why it helps to review afterward, to ensure that nothing is missed.

Now it's time to practice on the materials gathered for the drills. There is no need to reread these materials, since by now, they've been read several times. Simply try to recall the content, then review to gauge how completely you remembered everything.

In the beginning, recall can be aggravating. While attempting to trigger memory, the mind draws a blank . It knows what was read, but in the moment, it doesn't want to work on retrieving it. Trying harder only raises the aggravation.

If you can push past the mind's resistance, the next challenge is that you can't articulate the content as effortlessly as the author . This occurs because you've likely never practiced the art of recall.

Recall, as you've hopefully gathered from this drill, requires plenty of practice. It must be done repeatedly to integrate it into a habit. In the beginning, it will feel like the memories have to be pried out of your mind. Overtime, the need to pry fades and eventually disappears.

As explained, the mind slowly realizes that the information will be requested later, and so, it works increasingly harder to pay attention and remember while reading. The more you exercise recall, the harder the brain will work, and the stronger concentration and memory will become.

You don't even have to focus directly on improving concentration and memory in order to strengthen and enhance them. You simply need to work consistently on recalling and reviewing information you read, hear, and see, and memory and concentration will improve on its own.

In order to recall what we read, we must pay attention. But a devious little habit called daydreaming can get in the way of our ability to concentrate. The next chapter discusses the disruptive nature of daydreaming and ways to manage it.

Chapter 14 – Visualize

Reading is an active, imaginative act —Khaled Hosseini

Hopefully, I have succeeded in demonstrating that speed reading is about making slight shifts in habit that speed you up while reducing habits that slow you down. This book covered many habits that slow you down, such as fixation, regression, and subvocalization. There is one more habit that slows reading, and that is daydreaming.

We all fall into daydreams at one time or another. It often happens during activities that are relaxing or activities that we dislike or would rather not be doing . . . such as reading. Too often, the mind wanders, thinking about being on vacation, winning the lottery, or becoming king or queen of our inner circle.

Truth be told, daydreaming and getting lost in other thoughts might present the biggest hurdle to reading. When lost in other thoughts, the mind is everywhere *except* on the material. It becomes easy to read for hours and hour and not make sense of a single sentence. Although the eyes see the words, none of it registers because the mind is occupied on the daydream.

Everyone experiences these moments, some almost daily. In truth, I wouldn't be surprised if you were daydreaming or thinking about other things right now.

It goes without saying then, that to improve concentration, and therefore, comprehension and memory, you want to limit daydreams while reading. The problem is that daydreaming, like many processes inside the mind and body, is not under conscious control. It just happens. An idea in a sentence triggers a thought or image in the mind, and without consciously realizing that daydreaming has started, we are carried away. We may not realize that we are lost in the dream until much later.

Although everyone is prone to daydreaming, it occurs more with some people than others. Some are wired in such a way that they can't stop fantasizing. Day in and day out, they journey from one fantasy to another. If you are one of these people, it's likely affecting more than just your reading. It's not that you don't *want* to pay attention; it's that the mind won't allow you to process anything beyond those mental images.

Since we're not able to eliminate daydreaming completely, the best thing we can do is learn to manage it through visualization. Visualization is the act of forming images in your mind. It's similar to daydreaming, except instead of letting the mind run the images, we sit in the director's chair and take conscious control of the scenes.

Though, instead of creating random scenes, you sketch images expressed by the words you're reading. When reading a novel, for example, you visualize the characters, the scenery, and everything that happens to the characters just as the author describes. If reading about a process, visualize each step or phase of the process from beginning to end. If, on the other hand, the material is a tutorial or instruction manual, visualize exactly how each step should be performed. This is the essence of visualization during reading.

Keep in mind the goal is to visualize and read at the same time. So, form mental images of sentences as you read them. Do not wait until the sentence, paragraph, or passage ends to begin visualizing—simply allow the two activities to occur simultaneously. Also, do not stop at each sentence to complete the image, but move from sentence to sentence, forming images along the way.

As you might expect, this can be challenging. Truth be told, its more challenging than any of the other techniques in this book. Forming an image while reading forces the mind to perform two unique activities at the same time. The brain must make sense of words, and at the same time, create a visual of the words' meanings.

If you are not used to doing both, it can be overwhelming. You may experience fixation, regression, and brain knots as you figure out how to picture a particular sentence. As challenging or overwhelming as it may initially seem, the skill can be learned quite quickly if you take it one step at a time, which is what you will learn in this chapter.

Developing Visualization Skills

The following instructions will walk you through the process of building up the skill of visualizing written material. With practice, you'll develop the ability glide along text as images form instantly in your mind.

Words

Let's begin with something easy, visualizing single words. The following table lists 60 words. As you look at each word, create an image in your mind. For example, the first three words in the list are *dog* , *phone* , and *painting* , so create image of a dog, then a phone, and after, painting.

Do this quickly. Look at a word, quickly create a mental image, and move to the next word.

dog	lake	fill	broken	money
phone	man	neat	splash	fire
painting	door	aunt	meteor	deep
hoof	flee	diamond	dish	nail
flower	wheel	nose	house	dirty
bumper	square	nut	ant	fast
mend	desk	truck	faint	star
tooth	wing	kite	far	building
corn	board	run	neon	glass
feather	dust	brush	rust	lamp
bottle	computer	tree	boat	bowl
curtain	button	hat	sunset	mentor

That wasn't so bad! As you saw, visualizing isn't too difficult and can be done rather quickly. Though practice is key. To practice on more words, please visit: mindlily.com/speedreadingwords

Phrases

Next, move to visualizing multiple words. Below is another table, though this one lists word pairs. Create a visual image of each pair. As before, do it quickly, look at the word pair, visualize the pair, and move to the next pair.

red brick	pot roast	green apple	fried chicken
brick house	roasted almond	apple pie	chicken farm
house party	almond milk	pie chart	farm shed
white goose	sweet honey	broken glass	garage door
goose neck	honey bee	glass ceiling	door key
neck tie	bee hive	ceiling fan	key pad

Sentences

Let's take it up a notch and visualize sentences. Read the following sentences and mentally picture the action that is described.

Jeanne picked the red button

John drove by in a blue sedan

The branches blew in the wind

Coffee spilled all over her dress

Kyle forgot his sweater at home

Ice cold drink on a hot day is refreshing

Look at you, you're already visualizing sentences. Again, it helps to practice on more than the sentences offered here. For additional sentences, please visit: mindlily.com/speedreadingsentences

Fiction

Once you've practiced on randomly generated words, phrases, and sentences, the next step is to practice with works of fiction, such as novels or poetry. This type of work tends to be highly descriptive, which translates easily into visual images. In fact, such literature naturally lends itself to being visualized. Images will automatically appear, like a movie, right in your head and all you have to do is allow them to form as you read.

News Articles & Reports

When visualizing fiction becomes comfortable and natural, move on to news articles and reports. Even though news is factual, journalists present these facts in story form, thus why they are called *news stories* . Since they are presented like a story, they usually contain descriptions that are easy to visualize.

The goal when reading news stories is to picture the events and incidents being described. If a story reports a fire at a suburban lake house in which 3 people were rescued, picture a burning house by a lake with firefighters rescuing the 3 residents.

History

The next level up is history. Much like news, history tells stories, except these stories are about the past. Think of history as outdated news. Historical information is often presented in a less exciting, mechanical fashion, but these accounts still contain elements that are easy to visualize.

For example, when reading about Rome, picture where the empire first came into being and how it spread throughout Europe, parts of Asia, and Africa. Replay the major events and battles as described, and imagine how they shaped the empire. Visualize the different leaders such as Caesar, Augustus, or Constantine to power, giving orders, leading armies, and setting policies.

Science

History segues nicely into science. You wouldn't think science to tell stories or have descriptive elements, but they do. Though science stories are a little different and not quite as apparent. To some, they may not be so interesting either.

Nevertheless, science offers something that other types of writing do not. It describes parts and processes, like parts of an atom, cell, and ecosystem or the process of condensation, digestion, and photosynthesis. These are easily visualized by seeing the various parts and how they come together as a whole, or picturing the steps and how they flow from one to the next.

For instance, when reading about the organs of the body, you would picture where each organ is located and the function it performs. See in your head the heart pumping blood, the stomach digesting food, and the liver breaking down toxins. Also, mentally sketch how those organs interact with one another.

If reading about plants, visualize the process plants use to convert sunlight into energy or the route water travels from a plant's roots through the stem and up to its leaves and buds. As additional information is provided, insert it into the mental movie.

Practicing with materials in this order will help you adjust to reading and visualizing simultaneously. Again, visualization takes practice. You'll have to practice on a significant amount of writing before the act of smoothly translating written words into verbal images becomes natural. It's well worth the effort because visualizing while reading provides a host of benefits beyond managing daydreams.

First, it helps you engage with the material. The standard approach to reading involves staring at black text against a white background, which can get boring—and fast. That black text can also start to jumble together and sound similar. Visualization, on the other hand, gives life to text, making it vivid, colorful, and above all, real. Instead of passively absorbing information, you are actively involved, and at times, even experiencing the material firsthand.

Second, visualization enhances memory. As explained, vision is our primary sense and the majority of the brain's power is used to process visual information. This applies to memory as well. It's much easier to remember pictures than words. Many of our strongest memories are of visual experiences.

Finally, and most importantly, visualization aids comprehension. We've all heard the maxim a *picture is worth a thousand words*. That's because pictures are the language of the mind. Seeing something goes a long way to understand it, much more so than merely reading or hearing about it. If you can translate words into images, comprehension of written material will soar.

Practice Drill

Reread this chapter using the technique of visualization. Read a sentence and try to visualize it. Then, read the next sentence and visualize that. Move from one sentence to the next sentence, creating a mental image or movie the words describe.

You may find that not every sentence lends itself to being visualized, so you will have to get creative and take leaps in imagination. If a sentence doesn't automatically conjure an image, sit with it until it does.

If you are unaccustomed to visualizing while reading, read the sentence first before visualizing it. After becoming accustomed, read and visualize simultaneously. Then, go back over the sentence a few more times quicker and quicker each time.

Review this chapter several times, adding the skills practiced in previous drills: Space Reading or chunking, employing peripheral vision, and reducing subvocalization, fixation, and regression.

The next, and final, chapter moves away from speed reading and on to the very thing that makes reading possible—the eyes. The chapter will enhance your awareness about how much work these organs do, the level of respect they deserve, and ways to maintain their longevity to ensure many healthy years of reading to come.

Chapter 15 – Eye Health

The eye is the jewel of the body –Henry David Thoreau

Most of us take for granted how hard the eyes work and everything that they do. The eyes labor nonstop to help us see and make sense of the world. This includes making sense of words, whether in a book, magazine, text message, billboard, or flyer.

To do this, the eyes are in constant motion; moving up and down, side to side, backward and forward, as well as fixating and jumping numerous times per second.

Given all the eyes do, they can get overworked and tired. Therefore, it's crucial to take care of them. That includes stretching and strengthening the muscles of your eyes, relieving strain and stiffness in and around the eyes, and making sure they get the oxygen and hydration they need.

This chapter presents exercises to keep the eyes in tip-top shape. They are simple—simpler than any other exercise in the book—yet important at giving the eyes the maintenance they need. Doing them daily will improve the strength, flexibility, and range of motion of your eyes.

And strong, flexible eye muscles go a long way toward better reading. You will focus better, capture more text in a single glance, make precise stops, experience less strain, and as a result, move through text quicker. Eye strength and flexibility are essential to performing all the movements necessary to increase reading speed and expand peripheral vision.

Eye Exercises

Exercise 1 – Left and Right

Straighten your back, relax the shoulders, and look forward. Without turning your head, move your eyes, and look as far to the right as possible. Pretend you are trying to get a glimpse of your right ear. Hold there for one second.

Now, slowly move your eyes in the opposite direction. While keeping your head straight, scroll your eyes as far to the left as possible. This time, try looking at the left ear. Hold for one second.

Perform this right-to-left, then, left-to-right motion 10 times without moving your head.

Exercise 2 – Eye Roll

With head facing forward again, gaze up at the ceiling. Rotate your eyes clockwise rolling them to the right, then down, left, and back up toward the ceiling to make a full circle. Try to be smooth and fluid in your movements as you notice objects in the furthest corner of your peripheral vision.

Do this in reverse. Rotate the eyes counterclockwise by looking left, then down, then to the right, and finally, back to the top.

Repeat each direction 5 times, exaggerating the movement to stretch those muscles as much as is comfortably possible.

Exercise 3 – Figure 8s

Look straight ahead and make figure-8 motions with the eyes. Starting from the center, move your eyes up and to the left. Next, round the eyes to the top and down to the right. Bring them back to the center to start the bottom half.

Move the eyes down and to the left, round down to the bottom, up to the right, and back to the center again. As with the previous exercise, do this in both directions, and repeat each direction 5 times.

Exercise 4 – Plus sign

1. Look straight ahead.

2. Move the eyes to the left then back to the center.

3. Move the eyes to the right then back to the center.

4. Move the eyes up and back to the center again.

5. Move the eyes down, back to the center once more.

6. Repeat 5 times.

Exercise 5 – Scream and Squeeze

Open your eyes and mouth as wide as possible as if you are screaming. Allow all the muscles in your face, such as your lips, cheeks, forehead, and jaw to get a deep stretch. Hold for 3 seconds.

Now, squeeze the eyes and mouth shut as tightly as you can while also tightening the muscles in your face, neck, forehead, and jaw. Hold for 3 seconds.

Repeat this exercise 5 times. Remember that all of the muscles in the face are interconnected, so stretching the face muscles indirectly releases tension in the muscles around the eye.

Exercise 6 – Blinking

Sit comfortably in a chair, keeping your shoulders relaxed as you look directly at a blank wall.

Close your eyes, and hold them closed for half a second. Then, reopen them.

Do this 10 times.

Exercise 7 – Eye Massage

Sit straight, relax your shoulders, and close your eyes. Take your index and middle fingers and place them gently over each eyelid.

While applying light but firm pressure, gently move the right fingers in a clockwise direction and left fingers in a counter-clockwise direction. Repeat this circular massage motion 10 times. Then change directions for another 10 repetitions.

Once finished, use your fingers to massage the bones around the eyes, including the eyebrows. Again, apply light but firm pressure with your index and middle fingers while making circular motions.

Eye Breaks

In addition to doing the above exercises daily, give your eyes regular breaks throughout the day. Staring at text for long periods dries out the eyes, as they don't blink as often as they should. It also weakens their muscles. This causes the eyes to work harder to maintain focus and even to remain open. Taking regular breaks, even if momentary, gives the eyes a much-needed recovery.

Instead of reading or sitting in front of a computer for hours on end, stop every hour or so and disengage for a few minutes. In that time, avoid looking at text or at a screen of any type or size. Instead, stand up, walk around, and grab a glass of water or even a snack.

In addition, direct vision on an object about 20 feet away. If it helps, gaze out the window. Maintain that focus anywhere from 20 seconds to 2 minutes. Refrain from moving your eyes during that time as doing so defeats the purpose of the exercise. Simply focus attention on an object in the distance.

Simple eye breaks like these, taken throughout the day, give the eye time to relax, and when they're relaxed, they're less likely to become strained.

These are a few ways to relax and strengthen the eyes. Although they are not meant to correct eyesight, you'll find that after doing them, your vision is clearer. Another benefit of the exercises is that they significantly reduce headaches, migraines, muscle pain, and dry eyes associated with concentrating and focusing on tasks for extended periods.

Repeat the exercises at least once a day. You don't have to do every exercise every day, but choose one or two for each session. I do one exercise first thing in the morning and another before going to bed. Throughout the day, I do them as needed to relieve and refresh my eyes. If you do the same, you'll find that your eyes will feel stronger and better equipped for the constant stream of text that they encounter on a daily basis.

Conclusion

Congratulations, you've reached the end of the book!

As promised, speed reading isn't a difficult activity.

It involves shifting from looking at individual words to looking either at spaces between words or combination of words while keeping the inner narrator silent.

To further enhance speed, reduce the length and number of fixations, eliminate regression, and expand visual awareness, and voila, you're reading multiple times faster than ever before.

If you remember, Chapter 13 discussed the need to perform review and recall. If no action is taken to remember what was read, the majority of it will be forgotten within a few hours. All that will be left is a feeling that you remember the information.

Let's do some recall and review now so the lessons stay fresh.

Start with Section I. Think about the topics discussed in the three chapters of that section. Was there something that stood out as particularly important or that made an impact on your thinking or reading method?

Think also about the concepts you disliked. Did you find something annoying —something that you already knew or heard before? Don't disregard the areas that you resist or find annoying, because they offer important clues to growth and development.

For example, if you disliked the chapter on building vocabulary, it might be because you struggled with vocabulary in school, don't feel capable of having a strong vocabulary, or you simply dislike studying definitions. The areas we resist in life often present challenges that we are not ready to face or feel capable of confronting.

Do this level of recall and review for the 5 sections in this book. Do you remember all of the sections? Or the chapters within the sections? What about the exact order of the chapters?

Once you recall the chapters, think about the content. What were the major points, lessons, or techniques discussed in each chapter? How were they discussed, and in what ways did the details support the main, overarching topic? How about the instructions, exercises, and drills each chapter presented?

Do your best to recall as much as possible. Recall deepens the neural pathways to memories stored in the brain. The more you recall a fact, the deeper those pathways become, and the longer you are able to hold on to them. So, work really hard to recall everything. The more of the lessons you can recall in this moment, the longer it will stick, which means the more you will remember to put into practice.

A good way to aid recall is to think about information that is related to, or discussed, in close proximity to what you do remember. If you can elicit memory of chapter 8 on regression, can you elicit the chapter that came before or after it? If you remember *Exercise 2 – Eye Roll* in chapter 15, can you remember the other exercises? What about going a step further and reciting the instructions of those exercises?

Using what you do remember is a great way to trigger or aid recall of other items. So, when you have difficulty calling up what you read, try to remember any fact, element, or detail and use that to springboard memory of similar facts and details.

Once you recall everything, go back through the book to verify whether or not your memory is complete and accurate. You probably won't remember everything. There will be areas that you miss, which is to be expected.

As we've learned, the mind often holds a thought just long enough to understand the next sentence or paragraph. This makes it nearly impossible to remember everything in one pass. As the author of this book and someone who teaches memory improvement, even I am unable to recall the details of every chapter. So, it's important to go back and review the material to make sure that your memory is accurate.

Now that your memory of the lessons is strong, it's time to put the information and techniques to use. Choose a chapter and focus on developing the skill taught in that chapter.

It's not necessary to do this in order—begin with a chapter that you found challenging or one that will offer the most benefit. You might even start with one that is easy just to encourage yourself to begin. Then work up to the difficult material.

Either way, don't wait for a reading assignment to practice these skills. Repeat the exercises in the chapter over and over again until you master the technique. Remember from the introduction, practice is essential for integrating the techniques into your reading routine. Otherwise, the moment you pick up a book, old habits will take over.

Once the old behaviors are engaged, it's difficult to disengage them. You'll make excuses by saying that you'll apply the techniques next time, with the next material, or in the next session. You will likely make the same excuse the next time, and the time after that, until you forget much of the information you learned here. It's a common pattern that prevents progress.

That's how sly and devious habits are in keeping people in old patterns and routines, even when those habits admittedly don't work for them or when better options exist. So, practice every chance you get, and you too will master the art of reading a 200 page+ book in one hour.

The key takeaway is practice, practice, and practice!

www.ingramcontent.com/pod-product-compliance
Lightning Source LLC
Chambersburg PA
CBHW081621100526
44590CB00021B/3548